The Young Country Doctor: Book 6

# BILBURY PIE

## (Tales from the village of Bilbury)

## Vernon Coleman

ISBN 9781082143472

Bilbury Pie, a collection of short stories, is the sixth of Vernon
Coleman's books about Bilbury. All are available as Amazon Kindle
Books and as paperbacks. If you enjoy the Bilbury books you may
enjoy other books by the same author including *Mr Henry Mulligan*,
*Second Innings*, *It's Never Too Late* and *Mrs Caldicot's Cabbage
War*. For full details of over 100 books by Vernon Coleman please
see his author page on Amazon or http://www.vernoncoleman.com/

# GONE BUT NOT FORGOTTEN

When old Farmer Henshaw died last Wednesday it seemed to mark the passing of an era. I doubt if we shall ever see his like again.

Farmer Henshaw (I don't think anyone knew his first name and I doubt if anyone in the village would have had the courage to use it even if they had known it for he was not what one would describe as an 'approachable' individual) was no ordinary villager.

In addition to whatever passing memories he has left behind he has, even in death, given us at least one reason to remember him for some time to come.

He is the first person from the village of Bilbury to have been buried standing up.

Throughout his life, Farmer Henshaw loved defending lost causes and championing minority interests. Few things gave him greater pleasure than making bureaucrats look silly. He fought everyone and everything though the fighting was, I suspect, done as much for the battle as for the victory.

He fought hard against the Parish Council's plans to build a new village hall after the Second World War. And then, when the plans were defeated, he helped Norman Jackson prepare the appeal. When the County Council wanted to widen the main road into Bilbury he lay down in front of the bulldozer which was due to take the corner off the copse at Softly's Bottom. Less than eighteen months later he led a petition demanding that the very same road be widened to make it safer!

The instructions in the old man's Will were clear enough, though neither Mr Willoughby, the solicitor who read them out, nor the two Henshaw boys would have been too unhappy if there had been any way of avoiding them.

(The Henshaw boys, both in their sixties but for ever to be known as the Henshaw boys, were always something of an embarrassment to their father. One works as an accountant in London and the other is a solicitor in the north of England. Most fathers would be proud of such sons. But Farmer Henshaw never really got used to the fact that his two sons put on suits when they went to work. In his view no man had a proper job if he could do it without a ball of orange baler twine in his pocket.)

At first the two sons tried to persuade the vicar that it wouldn't be proper to conduct a burial service with the corpse standing upright.

But after the vicar had made some enquiries he told them that there was nothing in the funeral service that said that a dead man had to be buried lying down.

Amos Tweed of Black, Titmarsh and Tweed, the undertakers in Barnstaple, said that he had never known anything like it, but that as long as someone was prepared to pay for designing a new type of coffin and digging a hole that was twice as deep and half as wide as normal he would not object.

So a carpenter was instructed to make the coffin and Peter Marshall from the village shop was hired to spend an extra six hours digging a deep enough hole. When Peter had finished, Thumper Robinson and Frank, the landlord from the Duck and Puddle, had to lift him out with a rope. (Peter was more than a bit miffed about the fact that although he'd had the foresight to pay the Culpepper boy to hang around in the graveyard to go and get help when he needed it, Thumper and Frank left him there for nearly an hour while they finished a game of pool).

Then they had to work out a way to move Farmer Henshaw from the Chapel of Rest to Bilbury Church.

Amos said he didn't think Mr Henshaw would mind being carried lying down but the vicar said he thought that if we were to enter truly into the spirit of Mr Henshaw's Will he should be carried upright, and so Patsy's father had the silage washed off his best tractor and towed the coffin behind on a hay cart.

It made a strange sight. A still rather dirty red tractor pulling an erect coffin followed by the largest entourage of mourners that anyone could remember seeing in Bilbury.

The moment of truth came when the coffin was lowered into the ground. It sank gracefully until coming to rest with a loud thud, the top eighteen inches still protruding over the top of the hole. Peter Marshall reddened visibly and, after the coffin had been unceremoniously hauled up, he was lowered back down into the grave to continue digging. The waiting mourners retreated to the Duck and Puddle.

So, in death Farmer Henshaw was as newsworthy as he had been in life and the story of his burial (and attempted burial) was carried prominently on the front page of the local newspaper. Farmer Henshaw would have been very pleased indeed.

But it was when it came to sorting out the old man's estate that the real fun and games started.

Everyone in the village knew that the old man had been worth a few shillings. At one time his farm had included well over a thousand acres of prime Devon pasture land and Mr Henshaw wasn't a man who enjoyed spending his money. When his two sons were young he used to work them hard all day in the fields and then, to save on housekeeping, give them sixpence each to go to bed without any supper. The next morning he'd get his money back, with interest, by charging them a shilling each for breakfast.

So when the will was read and the two sons found that they'd been left the house and its contents between them and no more than £350 in cash everyone knew that however dead the old farmer was he still had one last trick up his sleeve.

Where, wondered everyone in the village, had old Farmer Henshaw hidden his fortune? We all knew that he was worth more than £350.

For days the two sons searched everywhere they could think of. They searched every room in the house. They searched the barns and they searched the stables and they went up into the attics and they got themselves covered in dirt and dust and rat droppings by scrabbling about underneath the loose floorboards in the ceiling of the old coach house.

They knew that the money wouldn't be in a bank - their father had hated banks – but although they searched high and low they could find nothing of any great value.

Suspecting that the old man might have invested his money in antiques they got an antique dealer to come and inspect all the furniture but there was nothing of value to be found there. The paintings on the walls were cheap daubs, there was no hidden stamp collection and Mr Henshaw's old runabout was no classic car.

For a while the sons suspected that the wallpaper in one of the bedrooms might be original 'William Morris' and there was talk at the Duck and Puddle that they were contemplating bringing in an interior decorator from London to peel it off but then someone pointed out that Mr Henshaw had the room decorated three years earlier and that the wallpaper had been bought in a sale at the ironmongers in Lynton.

Eventually, the two sons gave up, called in an auctioneer and decided to try to make as much as they could out of their inheritance.

The house was packed for the auction. Attracted by the hope of a bargain there were people there from as far away as Torrington, Okehampton and Tiverton. There was even an unsubstantiated rumour that a dealer had come all the way from Exeter to look at Farmer Henshaw's old desk.

Basil Wishbone the auctioneer was hired to organise the sale and the sons couldn't have done better. Basil never misses a trick and had lot numbers pasted on everything that moved or could be unscrewed. Basil once got so carried away that he sold his own jacket, and at one country house auction he is reputed to have sold (separately) two half used bars of soap, half a box of cornflakes, a set of false teeth with a crack in the plate and the letterbox from the front door. He got a good price for them all too.

In the end the auction raised £17,000, which wasn't bad considering that there wasn't anything there which fetched more than £250, and Basil even managed to sell the carpets and the curtains to Tippy Knowles, whose husband runs Blackwater Pond Farm.

It was the curtains which caused the trouble.

When Tippy started to take them down from the curtain rails she found that someone had sewn coins into the hems to hold them straight. She assumed that they were pennies but a flick from Peter Marshall's penknife showed that they were gold.

Old Farmer Henshaw had hidden his fortune in the hems of his curtains. Every single hem contained dozens of sovereigns.

Now, of course, there's a huge row going on.

The two Henshaw sons are insisting that the gold coins are theirs but Tippy and her husband are holding firm and are planning to spend their good fortune just as quickly as they can.

# FASHION SHOW

The clock tower of Bilbury church has developed a nasty crack and the vicar has launched a fund to try to raise the £20,000 that the builders estimate the repairs will cost. I have been appointed a member of the fund raising committee and our first event was a fashion show which we held in the village hall.

Our original plan was to find a local dress shop prepared to provide the dresses and a little ready cash in sponsorship money in return for some goodwill and a little advertising. The vicar said that a similar event organised in nearby East Moulton had raised over £100. Gilly, Patsy, Anne and the bathukolpian Kay had all been press ganged to serve as models.

Unfortunately, the only clothes shop in Barnstaple which was prepared to cooperate turned out to be a shop called Flimsies. No one on the committee would admit to having heard of this store which, we discovered, specialised in entirely impractical underwear that no woman would wear if her main intention was to keep warm. Having heard a brief description of the sort of garments involved the committee felt that an advance inspection of the stock was necessary and the vicar and I were appointed to undertake this onerous task.

I had, I confess, seen one or two items of a similar nature in the past (entirely in the course of business you understand) but to the vicar this was entirely uncharted territory.

'What exactly are these?' he asked, holding up several items in black silk that must have weighed no more than an ounce between them. The manageress tried to explain but the vicar was clearly too shocked to take it all in.

'We can't get any of our ladies to wear those things!' he whispered as we hurried away. Sadly, I agreed with him though I felt that in a way it was a pity for if we had been more courageous we would have probably been able to raise our £20,000 in one solitary but glorious evening.

Eventually, we ended up organising a fashion show with clothes supplied entirely out of Mrs Bridgford's Rummage Sale stocks (stored in her garage in a series of large cardboard boxes).

Before the show started we were all overwhelmed by a sense of gloominess which bordered on despair. I had been appointed as announcer for the evening and I was dismayed to discover that Mrs Bridgford had produced from her garage a range of clothes for which the only honest adjectives were 'sensible', 'warm' and 'comfortable'. Everything seemed to be in solid, dark browns or blues and to be made of either serge or tweed. Pockets were invariably 'capacious' or 'spacious' and zips were 'stout' or 'sturdy'.

We made a real effort to overcome our handicap. At Patsy's suggestion everything that relied exclusively upon orange baler twine for fastening was excluded from the show and the vicar used two cans of air freshener to combat the pungent smell of mould which rose like a cloud from each and every garment (though given the fact that the all pervading smell of silage which usually fills the village hall is impossible to defeat this was probably a waste of time).

Kay, our exceptionally buxom district nurse, was the first of our models to step out onto the village hall stage. She wore a pink and grey houndstooth check suit in Harris Tweed and an off-white blouse with imitation pearl buttons. Both the jacket and the blouse were several sizes too small for her and there was widespread admiration for the strength of the cotton holding the buttons onto the blouse.

Since I had never sold a pink and grey houndstooth check suit before I had no idea at all what price to ask for it and so I invited offers. Ignoring one or two earthy suggestions which brought a flush to Kay's cheeks and put a twinkle in her eyes (and a blush to the vicars' already ruddy cheeks) I eventually found myself selling the suit and blouse together for £12.50, at least £12 more than I had expected. I found out later that Thumper Robinson and Frank Parsons had kept the bidding going up in ten pence stages in the belief that the longer Kay remained on stage the greater the chance of nature, in the form of Kay's bust, proving too powerful for science, in the form of cotton thread.

And so the fashion show became an auction and by the end of the evening we had raised well over £250 for the church tower restoration fund. As Frank, from the Duck and Puddle, pointed out this means that we now only have £19,750 left to raise.

'What a brilliant idea!' said Mrs Lovelace afterwards. 'Most fashion shows are packed with unwearable nonsense but your clothes were all so *practical!'*

# OLD BRASS TAPS

A couple of months ago, I arrived at the Duck and Puddle for a medicinal tonic and found Thumper Robinson sitting at one of the outside tables, carefully examining something that looked like an old brass tap. His pick-up truck was parked nearby. An empty pint glass stood on the table in front of him.

'Do you want me to bring you a drink?' I called to him, as I approached the pub door.

This was a silly question. Thumper wiped what I could now see really was an old brass bath tap on his jeans, and then casually tossed the tap into a large, stout, cardboard box. Then he grinned at me and nodded. The box, I noticed, was absolutely full of old-fashioned brass taps.

'Where on earth did all those taps come from?' I asked him, a few moments later. I put a pint down in front of him, sat myself down opposite him and took a long draught out of my own glass. It was a warm day and I was thirsty. 'And what the devil are you going to do with them?'

'They're from the Gravediggers' Rest,' said Thumper, mentioning a local pub in Braunton which we both know well. 'I've been helping to clear out some rubbish for Franklin Mynton. He's having the place restored.' Franklin Mynton is the landlord of the Gravediggers' Rest. He is renowned for his meanness.

I picked one of the taps out of the box. 'How much did he charge you?'

Thumper looked at me as if I were mad. 'He paid me to take them away!' He explained. 'He just wanted the rubbish clearing out'.

'They look too good to dump,' I said, peering down into the box, and rummaging around.

Thumper looked across at me. 'Who said anything about dumping them?' he asked, raising a quizzical eyebrow. He lifted his glass and half emptied it in a single, long, smooth movement.

I might have known.

Thumper doesn't believe in throwing anything away. He and Anne Thwaites live in a tiny cottage on the moors where every outbuilding and barn is stuffed to the rafters with things which just might come in useful one day. Thumper saves everything from old feed bags and leaky watering cans to discarded tractor tyres and dead batteries

I completely forgot about the taps after that. But when I called at their cottage yesterday morning I found Thumper giving the taps a clean with an old rag and a bottle of patented brass cleaner.

'Are those the same old taps I saw you with at the Duck and Puddle a few weeks ago?'

Thumper looked up at me, grinned and nodded.

I bent down and examined one. 'I'd hardly recognise them!'

'Good.'

'Have you found a buyer?'

'I'm not cleaning them because I like the smell of polish!'

'Have you sold them all?' It seemed strange that Thumper had the good fortune to find someone to buy every one of the taps he had rescued from the Gravediggers' Rest.

'Every single one,' nodded Thumper. 'I've sold them to some fancy interior decorator from London. Clarence or Timothy or something like that.'

'Good price?' I asked, though it was a superfluous question. Thumper doesn't sell anything to anyone from London without making a healthy profit.

Thumper grinned. 'Good enough,' he admitted.

'Lucky he wanted them all!' I remarked.

'He's doing up a pub,' explained Thumper. 'They want to make it look really old-fashioned.'

I didn't put two and two together until a day later. I had to go into Braunton to deliver a pile of old books that I had promised to donate to the Cat Protection League jumble sale and I saw Thumper's truck parked outside the Gravediggers' Rest. I sat and watched him lift a box full of shiny, brass bathroom fittings out of the cab and hand them to a lanky, weedy looking individual who wore designer jeans, a ponytail and a pink T-shirt.

As the lanky individual wandered away clutching what he obviously regarded as a precious purchase I wandered over and said 'Hello!' to Thumper who was busy counting a very healthy looking wad of notes.

Thumper was clearly surprised to see me. He looked almost embarrassed.

'Just sold those taps, I see!'

'Er... yes.'

'Was that the interior decorator?'

Thumper swallowed hard and nodded.

'Where did you say he was working?'

Thumper didn't exactly blush. I don't think Thumper has the physiological equipment you need to blush. But he got close to it. 'The mumblemumble mumble.' he said.

'Oh, The Gravediggers' Rest!' I said, nodding at the pub behind him.

Thumper, who had just sold Franklin Mynton his own taps, grinned sheepishly, winked and put a finger to his lips. 'Come on,' he said, 'I'll buy you a drink.' He looked over his shoulder.

'But not here,' he added quietly.

# THE HORSE RIDE

Although I have lived in the country for many years I have never ridden a horse.

I don't mind patting them and giving them sugar lumps and I am happy to confirm that without horses my rhubarb patch would be but a shadow of its present self but I have always regarded the absence of any clearly defined equine braking system as a discouraging factor. As far as I am concerned if God had intended me to ride a horse he wouldn't have invented the bicycle.

(My scepticism about horse riding as a sensible means of transport is, I suspect, at least partly inspired by an unhappy experience I had on a donkey on Blackpool sands at the age of six. I do not wish to say any more about this experience.)

Last week Thumper, Anne and Patsy all decided that it was about time I abandoned my childhood fears and learned a little about the joys of horse riding. Although this adventure was clearly carefully prearranged, I first heard of it in the Duck and Puddle on Saturday lunchtime.

'Sarah Knowlson at Burnt Oak Farm says we can take four of her horses out over Exmoor for the afternoon,' said Thumper. 'We can take a picnic with us.' Sarah and her husband run a riding school.

I mumbled something about having promised to take Patsy into Exeter.

'Patsy's coming with us,' said Thumper. He looked across at Patsy, who was sipping her usual tomato juice.

Patsy nodded and blushed. 'You'll enjoy it!' she insisted. She looked guilty.

'This is a set up!' I protested.

Patsy had asked me to keep the afternoon free, saying that she wanted to go hunting for a new dress in Exeter.

'We knew it was the only way we would get you on a horse!' said Thumper, grinning broadly.

'What about that dress you wanted to buy?' I asked Patsy.

'It's for Simon and Laura's wedding,' said Patsy. 'And that's not for another three weeks. We can go to Exeter next weekend.'

And so I found myself being press-ganged onto a horse.

I doubt if there has ever been a less enthusiastic prospective equestrian. As I drove to Burnt Oak Farm my one comfort was the thought that having a horse between my legs would at least stop my knees knocking together.

'She's not going to bolt is she?' I asked Thumper as Sarah pointed out the largest, most docile creature in her stables.

'Lettuce could bolt faster than that horse!' Thumper said. 'Put your foot in here...'

With some difficulty and a definite loss of dignity I eventually succeeded in clambering aboard. I was relieved to find that the horse and I were both facing in the same direction but I was surprised to find out how high up I seemed to be. The horse hadn't seemed *that* tall when I'd been standing on the ground. As I gazed around the others leapt onto their horses with sickeningly practised ease.

'Hold the reins like this,' said Patsy. 'And just tap your heel into her flanks when you want her to start moving.'

I looked at her. 'Never mind starting. How do I stop?'

The others looked at me and then at one another. No one said anything.

Very gently and slowly we walked our horses through a meadow and along by a stream. Apart from nearly having my head removed by a branch I didn't think I was doing too badly.

'Let's try trotting!' said Thumper, when we had travelled a couple of hundred yards. 'Just tap your heels like this.' He did something almost indiscernible and his horse shot off like a bullet from a gun. Patsy and Anne followed him. It looked as safe and as inviting as space travel.

I sat still and tried to make sure I didn't move. I was particularly worried about my heels and I tried to keep them well away from my horse. She, however, had a dislike of speed which matched my own. She stopped, lowered her head and started eating.

Once I had got used to the fact that the dashboard had disappeared I didn't mind this at all.

'Come on!' shouted Thumper from half a mile ahead. His horse sprayed clods of earth in all directions as it skidded to a stop and then turned round. 'Dig your heels in!' he shouted.

Thumper's uninhibited enthusiasm reminded me of a ski instructor I once had who ordered me to ski over the edge of a cliff and seemed surprised and disappointed when I responded by deliberately falling over and going down the hill on my bottom. 'Don't you ever get afraid?' I had asked him. 'Afraid?' said the ski instructor with a puzzled look. 'Vot iz dat?' He must have been all of 18-years-old. I kept well away from him after that. I never want to be taught any potentially lethal activity by someone who has neither the imagination nor the experience to understand the consequences of disaster.

'My horse is hungry!' I shouted to Thumper. 'You go on. I'll have to stop here.' Gingerly, I dismounted, wrapped the horse's reins around a nearby branch (just as I'd seen the cowboys do on the TV), sat down on the grass and took out my sandwiches.

'What are you doing?' asked Patsy, laughing, when she and Anne had ridden back to me.

'We came out for a picnic,' I said, defiantly. 'So I'm having a picnic.'

I think one should try most things once.

I've tried horse riding.

# BLACK ECONOMY

I have recently noticed a considerable increase in the amount of bartering going on in the village.

During the summer I regularly saw our village shopkeeper Peter Marshall swapping loaves of bread, mint humbugs and pipe tobacco for fresh free-range eggs, runner beans and freshly picked strawberries. Frank and Gilly who run our local pub, the Duck and Puddle, have been paying their paper bill with beer for as long as I can remember. Even the vicar has succumbed to the rules of the new rural economy. He told me recently that the going rate for a christening was four pounds of strawberries and that he charged three large sacks of potatoes for a wedding. Thumper told me that when Arthur Jackson was buried, the deceased's brother paid the vicar's funeral bill by repairing the leaky downpipe on the north side of the knave.

The habit of bartering suddenly came close to home this week when Willy Porter, who lives in Nettledown Cottage next to Norman Kendrake's stables, came to the back door to tell me that he could, if I was interested, get me a cartload of fresh horse manure to dig into the vegetable patch at Bilbury Grange.

I'm a firm believer in manure and was immediately interested. Dr Brownlow, who calls manure 'political rhetoric', on the grounds that both come from a horse's rear end, taught me that whether you're growing strawberries, rhubarb or broad beans horse manure beats all known chemical fertilizers hands down. Dr Brownlow has been an organic gardener for a lot longer than organic gardening has been fashionable. Patsy and I have a good supply of used straw from the sheep's stable but you can't beat horse manure.

'How would you like to pay?' Willy asked. In shops this question is usually designed to find out if the customer wishes to pay by cheque, credit card or cash but I had a pretty good idea that neither credit cards nor cheques were likely to feature on Willy's list of possibilities. Cash is as close as Willy likes to get to the banking system.

'What are the alternatives?' I enquired, rather hesitantly.

Like Thumper Robinson and Patchy Fogg, Willy has quite a reputation in Bilbury as something of a wheeler-dealer. I'm never sure how much to trust him. He once brought me a boot load of neatly chopped up firewood that was so badly infested with woodworm that I didn't dare take it into the house. I swear that if you kept still and put your head close to the wood you could hear the worm munching their way through it.

'Three drinking vouchers or lend Norman your mower for a couple of days,' said Willy with a toothless grin. To Willy a drinking voucher is a five pound note.

It sounded an irresistible offer so I knew I had to think about it carefully. The problem with bartering as opposed to paying by cash is that there are no hard and fast exchange rates and there is no real way of knowing whether you've done a good deal or been done yourself. This makes bartering a hazardous business. Once anyone in Bilbury acquires a reputation as a poor judge of a deal, the reward is eternal ridicule and cold contempt. In a more kindly society poor financial judgement might be regarded as hardly more heinous than simple generosity but in Bilbury any man who throws his money around is regarded as a fool. Two years ago a fellow called Rupert Jackson retired to Bilbury with a very healthy bank balance after selling his share of an advertising business in London. Being a naturally generous soul (and accustomed to London wage rates) he willingly paid well over the going rate for work in his house and garden. I warned him that he was over-paying but he didn't seem worried. I think he expected the locals to look upon him as a kindly benefactor. Instead they despised him for damaging the fragile local economy, hated his ostentatious wealth and treated him with contempt which they made no attempt to hide whenever he ventured into the Duck and Puddle. After nine months he sold up and went back to London.

'Delivered?' I asked.

Willy grinned and nodded. He knew the deal was on.

'OK,' I said. 'But Norman can only have the mower for one day. Or I want two loads of manure.'

Willy beamed at me. Five minutes later we had hammered out a deal. So, I have now become a part of the village black economy. Each day living in Bilbury becomes more and more like living in an Arab bazaar. If only we had their weather.

# TALL STORY

I was standing having a quiet drink with Thumper Robinson when two men I had never seen before came into the Duck and Puddle. The taller of the two wore a flat cap with a well thumbed peak. He limped slightly. Both men were in their sixties.

They ordered drinks and then took them to a quiet corner of the pub where they sat down together. The man who wore the cap took out a small wooden board and a pack of cards. The pair then quietly began a game of cribbage. It is years since I saw anyone play cribbage in a pub.

'That's Terry Collins,' murmured Thumper, who was standing next to me at the bar.

'Who's Terry Collins?'

'The guy in the cap.'

'But who *is* he?' I was puzzled. By the way Thumper had murmured his name I gathered that the stranger was something of a local celebrity.

'He shot down a German bomber during the War,' said Thumper.

'He was in the RAF?'

Thumper shook his head. 'He wanted to join but they wouldn't have him. He lost both legs in an accident when he was a kid.'

'So, how did he come to shoot down a plane during the War?'

'He was out hunting for rabbits one night when he looked up and saw a bomber overhead,' replied Thumper. 'There was a full moon and the plane was flying low enough for him to see the swastika on the wings. The pilot was having engine trouble and had got separated from his mates somewhere over Dorset. He was lost.'

'And Terry Collins shot it down?'

'With his shotgun,' Thumper told me. 'It was a lucky direct hit on the plane's one good engine. The pilot managed to land on the moors and he was captured two days later. Terry painted a small plane on the stock of his shotgun.'

I was very impressed.

'So, who's the chap with him?' I asked Thumper.

'That's the pilot,' said Thumper. 'Klaus Hoffman. He never went home. He was in a prisoner of war camp until the end of the War and then he got a job as a translator for a technical publisher in Exeter.'

I looked across at the two men. To the casual observer they looked like a couple of very ordinary farmers having a quiet evening drink.

'What are they doing here?' I asked Thumper.

'They've probably been buying cattle at the Blackmoor Gate auction,' Thumper told me. 'They run a small farm near Tiverton now.'

'Together?'

Thumper nodded.

'That's amazing!'

Thumper looked at his watch. 'I must be going,' he said. 'I told Anne I'd be home an hour ago.' He finished his drink, grinned and waved a cheery goodbye.

'Astonishing about those two, isn't it?' I muttered to Frank, the landlord, when Thumper had gone.

Frank looked puzzled. 'What do you mean?'

'You wouldn't think there was anything special about them would you?'

Frank shook his head.

'I'd like to meet them,' I said. 'Do you think they'd mind if I went over?'

'What on earth do you want to meet them for?' demanded Frank, clearly puzzled.

'Thumper was telling me their story,' I explained. 'About the War and so on. I'd like to write about them.'

'I don't know what Thumper's been telling you,' said Frank.

'But those two didn't have a very interesting war. Hubert spent it in the catering corps in Aldershot. Ralph was in the Home Guard.'

'But one of them is German,' I mumbled, 'and one of them has artificial legs. They wouldn't let him in the RAF... I saw him limp when he came in.'

'The tall one? Is that what Thumper told you?'

I nodded.

'That's Hubert. He's got arthritis in his knee. That's why he limps.'

'Don't they have a farm together near Tiverton?'

Frank grinned and shook his head. 'They're both VAT inspectors. They've been out here giving Peter Marshall his usual three monthly grilling.'

I truly hate it when Thumper does that. One of these days I'll get my own back on him.

# FREE WHEELING ON EXMOOR

Too many people who live in the country seem to take the beauty of their surroundings for granted, only ever seeing the varying beauty of the countryside through their car windows. I know people who have lived in North Devon all their lives who have never walked on the cliff tops at Mortehoe, never watched the buzzards circling high above the moors in Lorna Doone country and never walked along the banks of the river Lyn to Rockford.

It is too easy to become blasé about the wonders of this world though this is not, of course, a fault which is unique to those who live in the country. There are probably people living in Paris who have never walked across the Pont Neuf by moonlight, never picnicked in the Place des Voges and never wandered through the Marais on a Sunday morning.

Although I made a deliberate choice to live in Bilbury because I love it I spend too much of my life sitting behind a desk. I am therefore always ready to seize the opportunity to go outside and to enjoy the wonderful, calming nature of this very beautiful part of the world.

Last Saturday Patsy, Anne, Thumper and I put the clocks back twenty years and went cycling on Exmoor. Neither Thumper nor Anne had bicycled for years and they had to borrow old bicycles which had been rusting away in the shed behind the Duck and Puddle.

We drove out onto the road between Simonsbath and Lynton, parked Thumper's old Ford pick-up truck on the wide verge near Brendon Two Gates and set off onto the most romantic, most alluring moorland anywhere in the kingdom.

As we wobbled off along a dusty moorland track and headed towards Hoccombe Hill it took Thumper and Anne several hundred yards to gain the confidence they'd had as children. (It took them a little further to discover how to operate the rather rusty gears on their mounts).

But within a few minutes they had remembered just how joyful bicycle riding can be away from the traffic and with only the ponies, the cattle and the deer of Exmoor for company.

We pedalled up steep and rocky, rutted narrow paths, we coasted at breakneck speed down grassy, rock strewn slopes and we explored the heather of Brendon Common, Badgworth Hill and Malmsmead country; the ever romantic, constantly alluring backdrop for R. D. Blackmore's spectacular Lorna Doone saga.

We saw dippers and wagtails and buzzards. We watched plump partridge struggle into the air and we admired the shaggy, prehistoric looking cattle which browse alongside the Exmoor ponies among the heather. No cars, no queues, no charge for admission.

We splashed our sweaty hands and faces with water from a crystal clear stream and ate lunch in the sunshine with our backs leaning against a moss covered dry stone wall. Fresh crusty bread from the local bakers, still soft and warm inside; hunks of farm-made cheese; crisp, juicy English apples and home-baked scones, hardly cool yet from Anne's oven. We dozed and watched the birds and like children on a day out told each other tall stories of our narrow escapes among the ruts and rocks of the paths we had explored.

Afterwards we cycled back up and over Malmsmead Hill, towards Withycombe Ridge and finally to Farley Water; splashing through shallow puddles and racing one another along narrow sheep paths. Exhausted but relaxed and content we got back to Thumper's pick-up truck just as the day was beginning to cool and the sun was starting to set.

Back in Bilbury we called in at the Duck and Puddle for a drink.

'Someone was trying to get you this morning!' said Frank, scrabbling around under the bar for the note he had made.

'They called two or three times!' he added, finally finding and handing me a scrap of paper with a London telephone number written on it.

People I know often leave messages for me at the Duck and Puddle but I didn't recognise the number the caller had left. 'Did they leave a message?'

Frank shook his head but handed me the telephone. I dialed the number.

'It's Henry,' said a voice I recognised, 'where the hell have you been?' Henry is a friend who lives on the outskirts of London. Hampstead. Finchley. Islington. One of those brick- road-car-noise-dirt-stress places. 'You've missed a wonderful opportunity,' he told me. 'We had spare tickets for a Post Modernist Art Display at the National Gallery. You could have come.'

'I was out,' I said.

'You miss all the good things – being buried down there in the middle of nowhere!' said Henry.

'Oh no I don't!' I thought.

But I didn't tell Henry what I'd been doing. I didn't think he would understand.

# VILLAGE IDIOT

A generation or two ago every village had its idiot and every village idiot had to put up with all sorts of cruel ragging. These days we like to think that we are more compassionate and less openly hurtful but I have my doubts about that. It may be that village idiots are no longer openly laughed at but deep down our society is just as thoughtless as it ever was. My despair and my anger are fuelled each day by sad, new stories of prejudice, ignorance and abuse.

Take Michael, for example. He is 25-years-old and he is what society now calls educationally subnormal. He can read a few simple words and he can sign his name but books, magazines and newspapers are a mystery to him.

But what Michael lacks in intellect, he more than makes up for in compassion and in spiritual strength. There is a gentle simplicity to his world and I sometimes envy him his black and white values.

Michael lives on the Lynton side of Bilbury with his brother, Tom and his sister-in-law, Elspeth. His brother has a small farm and Michael helps to look after the animals. He has a way with four legged creatures. They trust him.

Although his father is dead, Michael's mother lives in Newton Abbott and for as long as I can remember it has been his simple ambition to travel down to the south of the county to see her by himself. Last week I met Tom and he asked if I thought Michael could manage the journey by himself. 'He keeps on about it,' explained Tom. 'And I keep thinking of excuses. But do you think he'd be able to manage it?'

I said I thought he would. There is a bus service from Lynton to Tiverton and a good train service from Tiverton to Newton Abbott. And Michael's mother's flat is no more than a quarter of a mile from the Newton Abbott station.

So, last Tuesday was chosen as Michael's big day. Tom and his wife took Michael to the bus station and Thumper, Anne, Patsy and I turned out to give him a cheery wave. Elspeth had made a huge pile of sandwiches and wrapped them in greaseproof paper and Michael clutched them to his chest as he waited for the bus. He had a flask of coffee with him too and its sweet and milky smell filled the air around him. I don't think I have ever seen any man so dignified. He looked proud and excited as he waited for his adventure to begin.

'Have you got your money?' asked Tom, who was clearly apprehensive.

Michael nodded, pushed his left hand deep into his trouser pocket and pulled out a battered black leather purse. He started to unfasten it but Tom put out a hand to stop him.

'When you get on the train just sit down and stay there. Don't move about.'

Michael nodded to show that he understood.

'He'll be fine,' whispered Elspeth. She reached out and squeezed her husband's hand. It was a big day for them all.

Two minutes later the bus drove out of sight with Michael waving furiously from the back window. We stood together and waved him goodbye.

By chance I happened to be in Lynton again a few hours later and to my surprise I saw Tom driving by with Michael sitting beside him. Michael, who should have been in Newton Abbott, was in tears.

I telephoned Tom as soon as I got home.

'What happened to Michael?'

'He got on the train at Tiverton without any problem,' said Tom. He sounded tired and depressed. 'But the guard had him taken off the train at Exeter and the police rang me to go and fetch him.'

'What on earth happened?'

'He bought an ordinary return ticket but got into a first class compartment by mistake,' explained Tom. 'He didn't know there were two types of ticket so when the guard shouted at him he got confused. He said I'd told him that he wasn't to move until the train got to Newton Abbott. When the train stopped at Exeter they called the police and had him thrown off the train.' Tom sighed. 'The guard said that four smartly dressed businessmen from London had complained that they hadn't paid the extra to share their first class carriage with a drivelling idiot and so he had to do something.'

Poor Michael. I felt anger as well as sadness when I first heard this tale. I still feel anger and sadness now.

# THE GENERATOR

Like most local farmers, Thomas Yattenden has a generator in his barn so that on those occasions when Bilbury is deprived of electricity he can still milk his cows, prepare his animal feed stuffs and see where he is going and what he is doing on dark winter mornings.

Last month Thomas replaced his 20-year-old generator with a brand new, state of the art model that is designed to switch on automatically the moment the supply from the national grid switches off.

Thomas was immensely proud of his new toy and he insisted on taking us all round to look at it.

'Just watch this!' he said, flicking his mains electricity switch into the 'off' position. The lights dimmed for an instant and then brightened quickly as the wonderful new generator burst into action.

'Marvellous, isn't it?' purred Thomas. There was much murmuring of appreciation and Thumper and I applauded quietly.

Just then the generator stuttered, coughed and stopped and the lights went out. One of the essential laws of thermodynamics is that machinery will always break down at the most inconvenient and embarrassing moment and Thomas, although not inconvenienced, was certainly embarrassed.

'Just give it a kick!' said Thumper, who has a sensitive feeling for all mechanical and electrical equipment.

Thomas shook his head sagely. 'I can't do that,' he said. 'This is sensitive equipment. I've got a number to call in Exeter. There's probably a loose connection somewhere.'

The man who came out from the supplier in Exeter arrived in next to no time in a van which had a flashing amber light on the roof. I've known ambulances take longer. He certainly looked very impressive. He brought with him a huge box of tools, an inch thick manual and a variety of testing equipment. He had screwdrivers which lit up like fairy lights, multicoloured gadgets that beeped and burped and a pair of neat blue overalls with his name emblazoned on the breast pocket. A row of coloured screwdriver tops poked out from his pocket.

He could find nothing wrong with the generator and announced, with some regret, that he would have to arrange for a technician from London to come and take a look.

'I suppose that means I'm going to be without my generator for a month,' said Thomas wearily.

'Oh, no, sir!' said the technician from Exeter. 'Our man from London will be here tomorrow.'

And he was, too.

He came in an even bigger van with an even bigger amber flashing light and even more equipment. He wore a smart three piece blue suit instead of blue overalls and he had a row of pens instead of screwdrivers in his pocket. He had his name printed neatly on a small, white plastic name badge that was pinned to his suit lapel.

He spent a whole day on the generator and seemed, so Thomas later told us, to have completely rebuilt the whole thing.

But he couldn't make it work, either, and although Thomas was impressed with the quality of service he was receiving he was getting a bit fed up with the fact that his expensive generator didn't work.

'We'll have to get someone over from the manufacturers in Germany,' said the man from London. He telephoned London on the radio phone in his van and made the arrangements. 'One of their top design specialists will be here tomorrow,' he told Thomas. 'I'll stay overnight. I'd like to find out what the trouble is.'

And so the next morning there was quite a crowd waiting at Thomas's farm when the German expert arrived. There was Thomas, and the technician from Exeter and the man from London and Thumper and Frank from the pub and Peter Marshall. I was there too, of course.

The German expert came by plane and train and taxi and arrived at about mid day. He was very casually dressed in a pair of beige slacks and an open necked shirt and he carried a small overnight bag with him. He had no tools and no overalls and no name badge. He grinned a lot and shook hands with everyone, walked over to the generator and, before anyone quite realised what he was doing, gave it an almighty kick.

The generator burst into life instantly and purred like a contented cat.

'When they're new they sometimes need a bit of help starting,' he said in faultless English. 'Shall we have a nice cup of tea now?'

# TROPHIES

Lionel won the Club Trophy at Kentisbury Golf Club last month and he has been unbearable ever since.

He came into the Duck and Puddle with the trophy cradled carefully in his arms and stood there nursing it for twenty minutes while Thumper, Frank and I had one of our occasional philosophical arguments.

Thumper had started the argument by claiming that a couple of years ago there used to be a sign on Lynmouth beach which said: 'Do not throw stones at this notice'. Nothing else. Just 'Do not throw stones at this notice.'

Frank said that even the council wouldn't be so daft as to put up such a stupid sign but Thumper said that he'd seen the sign himself.

Then Frank said that he'd probably *thought* it had said that but that Thumper's memory had undoubtedly been distorted by prejudice and wishful thinking and alcohol.

And that is when it all got very philosophical.

Thumper said that what people remember is the truth and that history is simply what people believe. He said the facts don't really matter at all.

Frank snorted and said that this was nonsense and that history wasn't history unless people could prove it had happened, so Thumper asked him if Danny Jenkins had really been arrested for tying the back bumper of a police car to one of the poles holding up the refreshment tent at the Agricultural Show in Exeter. Frank said yes, that was history and so Thumper asked him how he could prove it and Frank said he thought it was time we all had another drink.

'Let me get them!' said Lionel, putting his very conspicuous trophy down on the bar and pulling out his wallet.

'That's a nice trophy!' said Frank, rising to the bait for the sake of a pint. 'What did you get that for?'

With considerable pride Lionel explained. The three of us listened with rapidly diminishing patience as he explained how he'd escaped from a bunker at the 7th, used a niblick to put his second within a foot of the pin on the 10th and drilled a drive straight down the fairway on the 14th. It was tedious stuff - made even more tedious by the fact that none of us understood what he was talking about.

'I'll loan you the trophy for display!' said Lionel, accepting his change.

'Oh no, I couldn't!' said Frank, who clearly didn't want his pub cluttered up with Lionel's ugly silver plated trophy.

'No problem!' insisted Lionel, sticking the trophy in between a small plastic model of Johnnie Walker and a collecting box for a Donkey Sanctuary.

\*\*\*

Lionel is normally only an occasional visitor to the Duck and Puddle but for the last four weeks he hasn't missed an opportunity to call in for a drink and every time he's been in the pub he has insisted on telling someone how he won his trophy.

We have all come to loathe the bunker at the 7th for allowing him to escape and our combined hatred of the hummock on the 17th fairway which bounced his ball back into play would be quite enough to turn any ordinary hummock bright red with embarrassment.

But I think our ordeal may now be over.

Yesterday lunchtime Thumper arrived at the pub clutching a large sack which clattered ominously as he dropped it down onto the floor beside the bar. Without waiting for any questions he reached into the sack and pulled out an enormous range of cups and trophies.

'Brought you my cups, Frank!' said Thumper, lining his tarnished silver ware up along every available piece of shelf space.

'What on earth...,' began Frank. 'Where did you get all those?'

Lionel, who was as usual sitting close to his trophy, ready to describe the way he had won it to any newcomers, said nothing but stared open-mouthed at Thumper's impressive collection.

'There's a story behind every one,' said Thumper cheerily. 'I'll start telling my sporting history tonight!' He picked up one small trophy and cradled it lovingly. 'Mid Devon Open Darts Challenge Match 1967,' he said, reading out the inscription on the small plaque screwed to the trophy's sun-faded wooden plinth. He turned to Lionel. 'Being a sporting man you'll be interested in this!'

Lionel made gargling noises and looked at his watch. 'I really must be off,' he said. He muttered something about another appointment.

'Where the hell did you get all those?' I asked Thumper when Lionel had gone. 'Did you really win them?'

Thumper laughed. 'Of course I didn't. I bought the lot for two quid at a house auction in Torrington this morning.'

# JACK POND

Jack Pond is 35-years-old and schizophrenic. He lives with his mother and father in one of a short row of whitewashed terraced cottages down near Softly's Bottom.

Many people are frightened of schizophrenics. They assume that all patients with this disease are dangerous, potential killers.

But the truth, of course, is that most schizophrenics are quiet, peaceful, innocent and entirely harmless. Their torment exists solely inside their own heads and they are rarely of any danger to anyone except themselves.

Jack is probably the most harmless person you could ever hope to meet. I doubt if he has ever had an aggressive thought in his life, though for years he has been tortured by feelings of self doubt and the suffering he has caused himself is incalculable.

Jack has never had a proper job. He has worked on one or two farms during the summer months but he is nervous of animals and because he is rather forgetful no one likes him to be too close to any of the machinery so his usefulness as a farm labourer is limited.

'He tries hard and he wants to be useful,' said one farmer. 'But I don't have the time to keep an eye on him and a modern farm is a potentially dangerous place.'

Six months ago Jack's life changed when he was offered a job in a specially run small factory which had been set up in a nearby town by a group of volunteers. The small charity running the factory believed that by giving people jobs they could help build up their self-esteem and self-confidence. They wanted to find regular work for people like Jack who couldn't hold down a proper job and so, with the aid of a small legacy, they bought a lease on a small factory unit and got contracts to do a variety of light, routine industrial work - the sort of work that is often done by people working at home. Packing small toys in boxes. Screwing grommets to grommets. Putting twenty screws in a plastic envelope. That sort of thing.

Jack loved his new job. He had to get up at six every morning in order to get to the factory and his pay packet was only ever very light but he enjoyed his work very much for it gave him a real sense of purpose.

Instead of spending his days watching television he spent them with new friends. He took great pride in doing the simple tasks he was given with skill and speed. The hospital consultant looking after him told me with some surprise that he had never seen Jack behave so normally. He said that he was thinking of reducing Jack's daily medication.

Jack's job even had a tremendous influence on his social life. Together with a few of the other men at the factory Jack formed a football club. They didn't play in any formal league but they met every Sunday morning and played a fast, enthusiastic and surprisingly physical game on a public pitch.

And twice, Jack went out to the cinema with a girl he met at the factory.

But now Jack no longer has a job.

A team of social workers swooped on the factory a couple of weeks ago and decided that because Jack and his friends were vulnerable and were being paid very little they were being exploited. They recognised that the people running the factory were doing so with no intention of making a profit. And they acknowledged that without the factory Jack and his friends would, once again, be left with purposeless lives. But the officials insisted that the factory must close.

Jack does not understand. He is now very depressed. He is depressed because he has lost his independence. He is depressed because he has lost his weekly pay packet. He is depressed because his life no longer has a sense of purpose. He is depressed because he fears that he will lose touch with the friends with whom he used to play football on Sunday mornings. And he is depressed because he fears that since he will not see her during the day time his relationship with his new girlfriend will fade. Besides, without his pay packet he won't have the money for bus fares or cinema tickets.

He is not, I am afraid, at all grateful to the social workers who want to stop him being 'exploited'.

# THE FAMILY MAN

I shared a flat with Tim Leyton when we were both at medical school and he was, without a doubt, the most exciting, unpredictable and stimulating individual I'd ever met. So, when I got a note from him asking if he and his family could come down to the West Country for a few days I was absolutely delighted.

'You'll love him!' I told Patsy and Thumper in the Duck and Puddle that evening. 'He's the wildest, maddest fellow I've ever met!' I told them about the time that he had been stranded in the centre of the city, long after the buses had stopped running and without enough money to pay for a taxi. Tim had simply walked into the bus station, climbed aboard a doubledecker and driven himself home in it. The next morning we all awoke to find a large, blue number 57 bus parked outside our flat.

It was Tim, I remembered, who had persuaded the rest of us to help him put a mini car belonging to one of the consultant surgeons on top of the flat roof of the nurses' home. The consultant had to hire a crane to get his car back.

And it was Tim who somehow managed to move a council grit bin (complete with a full complement of grit) from its natural roadside habitat into the reception area of the maternity home.

Not wanting to frighten them too much I didn't tell them about the day that Tim used a fire hose and twelve packets of orthopaedic cement to turn the matron's kitchenette into a swimming pool. Nor did I mention the day that he and the senior anaesthetist's wife were found together absolutely stark naked in the linen cupboard on the men's surgical ward. Tim was the sort of medical student you read about in books and I awaited his arrival rather nervously.

He and his family arrived with us last Tuesday in a four-year-old muddy brown Volvo estate car, and the moment I saw him I knew that Tim was not the man he had been. He wore a slightly crumpled blue suit that made him look like an unsuccessful insurance salesman. He smiled at me nervously and we shook hands rather formally. His wife, Myrtle, wore horn-rimmed glasses, a sensible skirt and an equally sensible jumper. She had the sort of shape you associate with chutney and PTA meetings. And they were accompanied by an assortment of children of various ages.

'Do you mind if I just make a phone call?' asked Tim, while Myrtle tried to persuade some of the children to stop screaming.

'No funny business with ink or super glue!' I warned him, with a wink. He frowned for a moment, looking puzzled. 'I just need to ring one of my partners,' he explained. 'We're having the surgery rewired and I want to remind them to put an extra socket in my consulting room.'

I went into the living room. Myrtle had turned on the television set and she and the children were watching a cartoon programme.

'Shall we pop round to the Duck and Puddle?' I asked when Tim had finished on the telephone.

He looked puzzled.

'The pub!' I explained.

'Oh!' Tim looked across at his wife, rather nervously. 'We don't like to take the children into pubs,' he said.

We all sat down and watched the television. A two dimensional rabbit was chasing a two dimensional dog down an apparently endless road. The children seemed to like it and it kept them quiet.

'It's kind of you to put us up,' said Myrtle. 'We're having a conservatory built onto the house so we're trying to economise on holidays.'

We sat for another hour or so watching the television. Several times I tried to begin a conversation but I've had more fun talking to Jehovah's witnesses. All Tim and Myrtle wanted to talk about was children, private schools, double glazing, the price of soap powder and the mortgage rate.

In the end I felt that I had to get out of the house. 'Is there anywhere you want to go?' I asked. 'Anything you'd like to see?'

Tim looked up. 'I think we're all O.K. here, thank you.' He had opened and was reading a copy of the European Medical Journal that he'd brought with him. Myrtle was reading one of the supplements from the previous Sunday's paper.

I stood up. 'I'll just pop to the shop and get some bread,' I lied. 'I'll come with you,' said Patsy quickly.

'Has your wild chum arrived?' asked Thumper, when Patsy and I walked into the Duck and Puddle.

'We had to escape,' I grinned. 'I must be getting old. I can't stand the pace any more.'

# THE TRAMP

Geoffrey the tramp had been a part of Barnstaple for several years. As much as a fixture as the Pannier Market or Butchers' Row.

He lived rough; spending his days prowling the streets on the look-out for bits and pieces of useful debris and his nights curled up in a cardboard box. I never saw him begging but if people offered him money he would accept the gesture with a gentle graciousness. He had a long beard flecked with grey and wore a brown tweed overcoat. Even in summer you could hear him wheezing like an out of condition water pump.

Once, I chased away a few youths who had gathered around to make fun of him. Some time last winter someone poured petrol onto his cardboard home and set fire to it. Geoffrey suffered severe burns and was lucky to survive. Where does such cruelty come from?

A couple of weeks ago I realised that Geoffrey had not been around for a while. Concerned and curious I made a few enquiries.

'We found him dead in a building society doorway,' an unconcerned policeman told me. 'He'd been beaten and kicked to death.'

I felt sadness, anger and despair in almost equal mixtures. 'Who did it?'

The policeman shrugged. 'No idea. Kids probably.'

'Why?' I couldn't understand it. 'He couldn't have had anything worth stealing.'

'Probably just for fun.'

'For *fun?*'

No one seemed to care very much. In death, as in life, Geoffrey had passed by unnoticed. No one will mourn his passing. No one will seek revenge for his loss. There will be no recriminations. This is the twentieth century. Civilisation.

I wondered what sort of man he was, how he had come to end his days sleeping in a cardboard box and what sorrows, despair, frustrations and unhappinesses had ruled his life. I have spent much of the week doing a little detective work.

Geoffrey was born in Wolverhampton in 1942 and although his childhood seems to have been uneventful, the first half of his adult life was extremely successful. He loved motor cars and was a brilliant mechanic. He built up a very successful garage business. At the age of 27 he married and, at his wife's insistence, sold the garage and bought a fast food franchise. His wife didn't like the motor car business. She thought it rather 'dirty' and 'low class'.

All went well for ten years. Geoffrey got richer and his wife gave birth to two children. He bought a large house with two garages, a swimming pool and a tennis court and expanded his business. The dream finally soured when his wife took a fancy to a young solicitor whom she had met at her tennis club. She announced that she wanted a divorce.

Although he was guiltless Geoffrey freely offered to give her the house. But it wasn't enough. She wanted money. Her young solicitor lover insisted that Geoffrey turn all his business interests into cash. It wasn't a good time to sell and the bank took most of Geoffrey's share of the proceeds.

With the small sum that was left over, Geoffrey bought an old van and started again; living in a rented flat several miles from the smart home he'd had to sell. He couldn't afford the equipment he had needed to set up a restaurant, so he parked in a lay-by and sold hot dogs and hamburgers to lorry drivers. He was happy to have the work and his customers were satisfied. For a while it looked as though he would survive.

Then, one morning Geoffrey woke to find a letter from his wife's solicitor on his doormat. She had found out about his new business and she wanted her share of the income.

Geoffrey left his rented flat, abandoned his van and headed south. Through some primeval instinct he headed for North Devon where he had spent many happy childhood holidays. Ilfracombe. Combe Martin. Lynmouth. The names drew him to them as surely as a lamp will attract a fluttering moth. Geoffrey arrived in Devon with no possessions and no money. He had only sadness in his heart. He just wanted to get away. To hide. To forget and to be forgotten. And the rest is now history.

Geoffrey was still a young man when he died. I wonder how many of the people who passed his cardboard home ever even wondered about the tragedy behind the man.

# PROGRESS

I had lunch last Tuesday at the Gravediggers' Rest in Braunton. I confess I don't normally stray so far from Bilbury but I went at the invitation of a friend of mine called Ed Hunter whom I hadn't seen for quite some time.

Ed is a Director of Human Resources for an American company and he normally works in a city where the traffic jams are endless and the air so polluted that breathing is a dangerous business.

(To be honest I still get confused by phrases such as 'Director of Human Resources', though I know that such jargon is all the rage these days. I have heard army spokesmen refer to dead bodies as 'non effective combat personnel'. On the radio, I heard a housewife described as a 'life support consultant'. People over sixty are no longer 'old'. These days they are 'chronologically enhanced'. Dwarves are 'vertically challenged' and tall people are 'vertically enhanced'. Ed once told me that no one who works for his company is ever made redundant these days. Instead they have to endure 'management initiated separation'. I think I'd rather be sacked.)

Ed has always been a bit gadget conscious and was the first person I know to have a portable phone. Sadly, however, his gadgets don't always work. I know for a fact that he has not been able to put his car away in his garage since he had an electrical opening device fitted. His garage now resolutely resists all attempts to persuade it to open and his car stands out in all weathers.

Ed pulled a small computer out of his pocket as we sat down. He couldn't wait to tell me all about it. 'It's brilliant!' he enthused. He always gets excited about his new gadgets. 'It's an electronic notebook, diary and calculator all rolled into one.' Like most city folk he always thinks that just because I live in the country I live a primitive, rather backward existence. He pressed a couple of buttons and showed me my initials and telephone number on the computer's tiny screen.

'There you are!' he said, triumphantly. He suddenly sniffed as though his nose had been assaulted by some noxious smell. 'What's that?' he demanded.

I sniffed too. I couldn't smell anything.

I am not over keen on computers. I have an enduring suspicion that much of the time they offer answers to problems people don't have and wouldn't be bothered about solving even if they knew they had them. My idea of high technology is having a rubber fixed on the end of my pencil. I put my hand in my pocket, pulled out my old-fashioned pocket diary (29 pence in the January sales), opened it and showed my friend his name, address and telephone number.

'It's quicker my way,' I pointed out.

'You're such a Luddite,' he exclaimed. 'You'll have to buy another diary next year. My computer comes complete with a 199 year diary.'

I looked at him in quiet amazement. 'Why do you want a diary for 199 years?'

He had the good grace to look slightly uncomfortable.

'What appointments do you have for the year 2087?' I teased him.

He muttered something about long-term strategic planning and then wagged a finger at me. 'My little gadget will tell me the time in 126 different places all over the world.'

'How many places can you be in at any one time?' I wanted to know, genuinely confused and unable to discern a purpose for this excess of knowledge.

Ed was beginning to get angry. 'Now you're just being deliberately difficult,' he said. He tapped away at his tiny keyboard. 'There!' he said proudly, a few moments later, showing me his tiny screen. 'I've written myself a memo. When I get back to the office I can copy that out.'

He sniffed again. 'Are you *sure* you can't smell anything odd?'

I pulled a 20 pence notebook out of my pocket, found a stub of pencil and scribbled a memo to myself. As I scribbled I realised what the smell was. Silage. My shoes always smell of silage.

'Me too!' I countered, showing him my note.

'But your diary and your notepad are so ...,' he paused, searching for the right words, 'old-fashioned'.

'I know. And cheap.'

He suddenly bent forwards and peered at his new toy. He looked worried.

'What's the matter?'

'I don't know,' he said. He turned the computer round and showed me an empty screen. 'I think the battery might have gone.'

I offered him my notepad. 'Do you want to make a note to get yourself a new battery?'

# THE SHY ROCK STAR

His face appears on millions of record covers and on thousands of posters. Every night several hundred thousand young girls (and some quite a number of not so young women) say 'goodnight' to him when they go to bed. Once a year he goes on tour to America, France, Germany and Japan and his concerts around the world are sold out within hours of the tickets going on sale. Last year the group of which he is a member earned rather more than Wales.

Despite all this success he lives in Bilbury in total obscurity. Without his long, blond wig and flamboyant clothes he is never recognised. He drives an old, beaten up, muddy Land Rover and invariably wears wellington boots, a green waxed coat and a flat cap with a grubby peak. He lives in two small silver miners' cottages which were knocked into one half a dozen years ago by a local builder. He has a horse and a Great Dane and shares his life with a good looking, plumpish girl who always wears tight fitting blue jeans and dark coloured sweaters.

I'm not going to tell you his real name (which is the name he uses in Bilbury) or his stage name (which you would recognise instantly) because he works hard at keeping the two parts of his life quite separate.

He has lived in Bilbury long enough to be a part of the village and he gives of his time quite freely. Last summer he helped Thumper and me clear the village pond; spending two days up to his waist in stagnant water and helping to fill the skip we had to hire to carry away the old bicycle frames, pushchairs, prams, flat irons and pieces of motor car which had been dumped in the water. (We even unearthed two shopping trolleys despite the fact that the nearest supermarket is probably across the Bristol Channel!)

Most people in show business pretend to want privacy but then do everything they possibly can to ensure that their private lives are made public. 'People who buy houses in Marbella and spend their free time going to nightclubs and beach parties don't have any right to complain if they find themselves being chased by photographers.' says Bilbury's gentle rock star.

He claims that public figures who cavort in public places have abandoned their right to privacy and argues that anyone who wants a private and peaceful life can have one easily if only he (or she) is prepared to find their Bilbury and then spend time living there.

'Most of us dress ourselves up so much when we're working that we're virtually unrecognisable when we're not on stage,' he says. 'And people who don't work in disguise could easily change their appearances enough to enable them to escape from journalists and photographers if they really wanted to.' He is living testimony to the truth of this assertion. On stage he is wild, unkempt and even frightening. Off stage he is shy, retiring and inconspicuous.

'Surgeons don't wander around dressed in gown and mask when they are at home,' he points out. 'When I'm working I dress up and put lots of make-up on. When I'm not working I'm a different person.'

Just before Christmas Frank and Gilly from the Duck and Puddle organised a trip to Wembley to see a rock concert. By chance they chose to see a show performed by a man who spends much of his life sitting in a corner in the pub they run. By irony they invited the star of the show they were going to see to join them on the coach trip.

'Sorry,' he said, when they told him the venue, the date and the name of the main attraction. 'I'm afraid I won't be able to make it then. I've got something fixed up.'

'It'll be a cracking show!' promised Gilly. 'I saw him in Birmingham last year. He was fantastic!' She had no idea at all that her hero was standing less than a yard away from her, dressed in a mud spattered Barbour and a pair of oil and mud stained jeans.

'Not really my scene, love.' said our rock star shyly. 'I'm a bit old for all that.' He emptied his pint and shuffled out of the bar. 'Really nice bloke,' said Frank, when he'd gone. 'But he needs to let himself go a bit more.'

Gilly looked at me. 'It's a shame,' she said. 'The funny thing is that X (she mentioned the name of the rock star) must be about the same age as him! You couldn't imagine two more different people, could you?'

I didn't say a word.

# NICE TO COME HOME

It isn't easy being a vegetarian. I see nothing odd in preferring to see animals walking about rather than sliced up with two veg or mashed up (bones, intestines, tonsils and all) and served up with chips, but some people still think that refusing to eat animals is a sign of lunacy.

It is, however, a darned sight easier being a vegetarian in Britain than it is once you leave the country.

I've just come back from a two day visit to Lindau in Bavaria.

I should have guessed that my stomach was in for a bad time when the stewardess brought me my in-flight meal on the aeroplane. I had, of course, warned the airline that I was vegetarian but the meal they had prepared consisted of cheese flan, cheesecake and cheese and biscuits. At least I think it did. Since I don't eat cheese I didn't actually taste any of the stuff in my little plastic dish. I ate the radish which was decorating the cheese flan and the two small biscuits that came with the cheese and washed down this unbalanced repast with a miniature bottle of white wine (for what it's worth, my advice is that no one with a sensitive palate should ever drink red wine on an aeroplane).

Seven hours later I was comfortably settled in one of the world's most beautiful hotels on the shore of a lake which is bordered by three countries (the Swiss call it Lake Constance, the Germans call it Bodensee and the Austrians call it Lake Konstanz and still the pro-Europeans talk of European unity).

The peace there is majestic: monasteries and castles cling to cliff tops, and hang in the mist, built as though to defy the possible and the practical.

I wandered into one of the hotel restaurants to order a meal. There were 59 items on the menu and with the aid of my fragile German and a small dictionary I worked my way through them all. If you exclude the one which my dictionary translated as 'Enclosure with deposit' (I hate to think what it was) no less than 58 of the available meals were meat based. I ordered the 59th: Russian egg and potato salad. It came covered in slices of salami. The Germans hate serving up anything that doesn't have a bit of a dead animal in it somewhere. I suspect they think they'll be arrested if they serve food that doesn't include meat. For dinner I ate two slices of black bread and drank two bottles of light beer.

Next morning at breakfast I decided to fill up with bread rolls. I sat at a rose laden table overlooking the lake and spread thick black cherry jam on a crisp brown roll covered with something white which I took to be sugar. It wasn't sugar. It was salt. I can still taste that roll and it makes me shudder as I write.

During the conference lunch break, obsessed with the thought of food, I wandered around the town looking for somewhere to eat. It was all typically Bavarian. Impossibly steep roofs, painted wooden shutters, colourful window boxes and neatly stacked piles of logs. I thought I'd got close to something promising fairly early on. The main item in the dish that had caught my eye was mixed vegetables covered in something that looked, even in German, like a misprint. It was one of those long, composite German words. I split the word up into its component parts and discovered that the mixed vegetables were served with a thick covering of bacon fat.

Eventually, I found a cafe which advertised soup of the day as consisting of tomato soup with rice. I ordered this. When it came it arrived with a large sausage floating in it. A huge dollop of fresh cream was balanced on the sausage.

On the flight back the airline served me a half decent vegetarian meal but brought no cutlery.

'I have no cutlery,' I pointed out, apologetic as only an Englishman can be under such circumstances.

'Yes,' said the stewardess with a smile. 'That'll be because you're a vegetarian.'

When I got back to Taunton I walked round the corner from the railway station to the chip shop just under the railway bridge. There I bought the biggest bag of chips they would serve me with and ate them in the street.

It's nice to go travelling but it's always nice to come back home too.

# PLEASE SHUT THE GATE

Tradesmen and delivery drivers have left open the main gate to Bilbury Grange on three separate occasions in the last week. As a result, wandering sheep have spent a very pleasant hour or two munching their way through our shrubbery, pelleting the drive and aerating the croquet lawn.

So, this morning I drove into town with the express intention of purchasing a 'PLEASE SHUT THE GATE' sign. It seemed a modest ambition.

The first shop I tried, a stationers, could only offer me a variety of small, red and white plastic stick on signs carrying such messages as PLEASE WASH YOUR HANDS NOW and DANGER GUARD DOG PATROLLING. I explained to the salesman that none of these messages seemed entirely appropriate and asked him if he would suggest anywhere else that I could try.

'You could try the shop four doors down,' suggested the salesman. 'It's run by my brother-in-law. Mention my name.' Foolishly, I accepted his recommendation and tried the shop four doors down. Although my confidence was not enhanced by the discovery that the craftsman who had designed and executed the sign over the shop had described it as a plumbing supplies centre, I suppressed the inevitable sense of pessimism that this discovery inspired and explained to the assistant, a tall, dour-faced youth wearing a grey smock and a sullen look, exactly what I was looking for.

'Your brother-in-law suggested I try here,' I told him, when my explanation was greeted with a blank stare.

The dour-faced youth continued to stare at me dully. His mouth had fallen wide open and I could see that a clumsy labourer masquerading as a dentist had at some time slapped vast quantities of mercury amalgam into his mouth. His teeth were silver rather than white and looked as though they had been repaired by a man with a grudge.

'Do you sell signs?' I asked him, speaking slowly and clearly, as though addressing a foreigner.

The youth continued to stare at me and I could see that he was thinking. This was, for him, clearly something of an adventure, a sail into uncharted waters.

'Signs.' I said. I looked around. My eyes lit upon the 'OPEN' and 'CLOSED' sign on the back of the shop door. I pointed to it to illustrate my message. The youth followed my outstretched finger and nodded slowly. 'My uncle does up and over garage doors,' he told me proudly and inconsequentially.

Eventually, I found a shop that sold signs. It was full of signs. I had never seen so many signs in all my life. There were signs of all shapes and sizes. Red and white signs. Black and yellow signs. Blue and white signs. PLEASE DO NOT GIVE ICE CREAM TO THE PEACOCKS. DO NOT THROW STONES AT THIS NOTICE. CARS PARKED BEYOND THIS NOTICE WILL BE UNDER WATER AT HIGH TIDE.

'Do you have a sign that says PLEASE SHUT THE GATE?'

I asked a man in a green tweed suit. He was wearing a pale yellow shirt and a red tie. He looked like a short circuited traffic light.

The man didn't hesitate. 'No, sir! I'm afraid we can't help you with that.' As he spoke he flicked through a clutch of ready-made signs and picked one out. He held it out so that I could read it. 'What about this, sir?'

I looked at it. It said: NO HAWKERS, NO CIRCULARS, NO TRESPASSERS. I must have looked disappointed.

'I didn't really think so. Sorry not to be able to help,' he said. Then he leant forwards, as though about to share something deeply confidential with me. 'It's a funny thing, sir, but we get a lot of requests for PLEASE SHUT THE GATE signs.'

'I'm not surprised.' I said. 'There must be a lot of people who get fed up with having their gates left open.'

'Exactly my sentiments, sir.'

'Why don't you make one?' I asked him.

'Sir?'

'A sign that says: PLEASE SHUT THE GATE.'

The sign salesman shook his head violently. 'Oh, I don't think the manager would agree to that, sir.'

'Why on earth not?'

'He keeps a strict record of which signs sell best,' explained the salesman. 'And we've never sold a single PLEASE SHUT THE GATE sign in the seventeen years I've been here.'

I went home, found a flat piece of wood and a pot of paint and made myself a sign. I may have found a market niche.

# PEAR TREES AND TIGER DUNG

Animals are invariably more intelligent than most of us realise. And they are equipped with extraordinary skills and talents.

Consider, for example, this remarkable true story of the deer belonging to Sir William Footling-Blenchard.

Sir William is the local Bilbury aristocrat. He lives in faded glory in what undoubtedly was, in the eighteenth century, a splendid castle but is today a rather run down and sad looking place. The battlements are crumbling, the roof is leaking and the whole place is held up by ivy, history and extensive strands of dry rot. There is hardly anything left for the woodworm to eat and the oak beams have been turned into fretwork by battalions of death watch beetles.

But however dismal Blenchard Castle may be inside it still has one remaining virtue: its gardens. Every summer visitors come in their thousands to walk around gardens which were once described in a Sunday newspaper colour supplement as 'the most majestic, the most inspiring and the most colourful private gardens in England'.

Some time ago Sir William realised that he could not afford to try to restore the house and to keep the gardens in good order. He had to choose one or the other and so without any apparent regret he moved into the two bedroom lodge house and chose to maintain the gardens.

Recently, however, Sir William has faced a problem that few ordinary gardeners will have ever had to worry about: his deer have been eating his pear trees.

To those gardeners more accustomed to worrying about greenfly or slugs, Sir William's problem may sound absurdly esoteric but to Sir William the problem was just as real as caterpillars eating the cabbages may be to the man with an allotment.

A fortnight last Tuesday, Sir William discovered a solution. Or, at least, he *thought* he had discovered a solution. Hearing that a cousin in Yorkshire, who had exactly the same problem, had found that if he regularly put buckets full of tiger dung around his pear trees the deer kept their distance, Sir William immediately contacted the Budleigh Salterton Wildlife Park and made arrangements for a small van load of fresh tiger dung to be delivered to Bilbury every week.

(There was, by the way, some immediate and rather intense controversy over whether tiger dung is subject to value added tax. One school of thought argued that tiger dung is inherently agricultural in content whereas another claimed that the provision of tiger dung is essentially a branch of the entertainment industry and a third group asserted that the tiger dung is being used as a security measure. A fourth group of accountants and customs and excise specialists supported Sir William's assertion that whatever its immediate purpose may be the tiger dung was inherently nutritious and should, therefore, be classified either as a foodstuff or as a fertiliser. This controversy is, I suspect, destined to run and run.)

Sadly, Sir William's high hopes for the efficacy of tiger dung as a deer deterrent were dashed when the deer ignored the buckets full of dung and continued to munch their way through the pear orchard, eating leaves, blossom, shoots and branches with undisguised and undiminished delight.

This failure puzzled both Sir William and his cousin but a telephone call to the Budleigh Salterton Wildlife Park provided a quick explanation.

It seemed that the two tigers in Budleigh Salterton had both been constipated for a week and so the game warden who had been given the task of collecting together a van load of valuable tiger dung had instead collected together a van load of lion dung.

When he was told about this substitution, Sir William's cousin snorted and then explained that lion dung just wouldn't do the job. When they had smelt the lion dung around the pear trees the deer would have sniggered quietly and knowingly to themselves and then gaily carried on munching the pear leaves. They knew that they could outrun lions and so they weren't frightened.

All has turned out well.

Now that the tigers are no longer constipated and Sir William's pear trees are protected by genuine, 100% tiger dung, the deer, who have never met a lion or a tiger but who instinctively know that they cannot outrun tigers, are sticking to the grass and leaving the pear trees alone.

# THE BAKERY

I love the smell of freshly baked bread.

Bilbury does not have its own bakery and so I usually shop at a small bakers in the next village where the loaves are freshly prepared on the premises every morning and where the sweet, warm smell of rising dough is a delightful daily bonus. On dry days I cycle there and back on my rather rusty old bicycle.

The shop is owned by a middle aged couple called Bristow. Helen, plump, blonde and nervous is the baker. She hardly ever ventures out from the small, hot, dark room at the back of the shop where she tends her ovens. George, her husband, looks after the shop and is well suited to it. He has a constantly sunny demeanour and greets each new day and each fresh customer with a never changing smile. I have sometimes suspected that if I had to live with him I might find George's never failing cheerfulness rather wearing. But as a customer I find his smile as warming as a ray of sunshine. Have you ever noticed how difficult it is not to smile back when someone smiles at you? And have you noticed how difficult it is to feel glum when you are smiling?

Helen and George, both native Londoners, met in a most unusual way.

Throughout her teenage years Helen had been prone to attacks of shyness and dominated by an almost overwhelming lack of self-confidence. She was overweight from childhood and was always self-conscious about her appearance.

In her early twenties Helen had to be admitted to hospital suffering from a deep, dark and seemingly impenetrable depression. The doctors who looked after her tried drugs, they tried electric shock therapy and they tried talking to her. None of these things worked and Helen's depression remained stubbornly incurable.

Eventually, one day, the inevitable happened. Helen tried to commit suicide.

Since the psychiatric ward in which she was a patient was on the sixth floor of the hospital and since the hospital administrators had never got round to putting bars on the windows Helen's choice of method was simple and straightforward. Early one morning she climbed through a window and threw herself out.

Eighty feet or so below she landed on the roof of a taxi belonging to George Bristow. The roof of the taxi caved in (hitting George's head) and instead of dying Helen was taken back into the hospital suffering from bruising, shock and embarrassment. George was taken into the accident department for X-rays and observation.

Two days later, when he was allowed out of bed, George visited the woman who had given him such a severe headache and for him it was love at first sight. He had always been over-endowed with optimism and happiness and he regarded Helen's persistently gloomy nature as a challenge to his cheeriness.

Much to the surprise of her doctors Helen responded well to George's daily visits and three months later she was discharged. They were married six weeks after that and although neither of them knew anything about baking or retailing they used a small inheritance of George's to buy our nearby bakery.

I usually call at the Bristow's bakery at roughly the same time every morning and for nearly a year I have watched George carefully breaking a brand new loaf into tiny pieces and then putting the pieces of crust into one brown paper bag and the soft, inside pieces into another brown paper bag.

I often wondered why George was doing this and I invented a number of possible explanations for myself. It was, I thought, possible that he might have a regular order from a restaurant wanting raw ingredients for a bread and butter pudding. Another possibility I toyed with was the fact that he might have an edentulous customer who needed his bread breaking up into mouth sized pieces.

Yesterday, I found out why George broke up a loaf every day and put the soft bits into one bag and the crust into another. I satisfied my curiosity by the simple process of asking George why he was doing it.

'It's for Mrs Garrow,' explained George. 'She likes to sit and feed the birds in her garden but she's got bad arthritis in her fingers and can't break up the bread herself. The soft, squashy bits out of the middle of the loaf are for the sparrows and the robins and the tits and the hard, crusty bits from the outside of the loaf are for the pigeons.'

# GEORGE AND SALLY

'I'm sorry to have got you up,' said George quietly. 'But I couldn't think of anyone else to call.'

I told him not to be so silly, muttered stuff about that being what friends are for and put my arm around him. He had been crying. His eyes were still red and puffy and his cheeks were tear-stained. There was something wrong, something missing, but for the moment I couldn't work out what it was. The long drive to the city had woken me up but now I was beginning to feel tired again.

I don't know what time it had been when the phone had woken me. I'd been fast asleep and for a moment or two I hadn't recognised George's voice. I suppose that wasn't all that surprising. None of us sounds entirely normal when we are frightened and George was certainly frightened. He is 84-years-old and it was the first time he had ever been in a police station.

I've known George for as long as I've lived in Bilbury. He lives alone, with a Border collie for company, in an old farm labourer's cottage. He gets his water from a spring and his electricity from an unreliable old generator which works on alternate Wednesdays when the wind is in the right direction.

I asked him what had happened.

'I went to see my sister,' he told me. 'She lives here.'

I nodded. I'd met her once or twice when she'd come to Bilbury for short holidays. A former school mistress she is five or six years younger than George.' She had an operation,' explained George. 'I came up to see her in the hospital.'

'What sort of operation?' I asked him automatically.

George looked puzzled. 'I don't know,' he said. 'I didn't ask.' It was not, I knew, because he didn't care but rather that he didn't like to ask.

'I came on the Bus and the Train,' he said. When he spoke he somehow made it sound as though there was only one Bus and one Train. This was almost certainly the first time for fifty years that George had been more than ten miles from Bilbury. For him it had been a brave excursion into a world he did not know. 'I was on my way back to the station when I met these boys.' The tears started to stream down his cheeks again.

'Boys?'

'There were a lot of them. Ten or fifteen at least.'

I turned and looked at the policeman who was standing silently in a corner. He was overweight, balding and had a nasty little toothbrush moustache parked on his upper lip.

'Football supporters, doctor,' the fat policeman explained. 'Their side lost,' he added, as though that both explained and excused what had happened. He was, I felt, the sort of man who hides behind his uniform, his job and his superiors but enjoys the power that goes with the uniform.

'They started taunting me,' said George. 'And Sally didn't like it.' I suddenly remembered what was missing. Sally. His 12-year-old Border collie. George would never go anywhere without her. They adored each other. I looked around but she was nowhere in sight.

'Where is she?' I asked him quietly.

George tried to speak but couldn't. The tears were pouring down his cheeks. I held him to me and waited. 'She started barking so they began to kick her.'

I went cold inside and looked at the policeman. 'What happened?' I demanded.

'They kicked the dog to death,' said the policeman. For a moment I thought that he was embarrassed then I realised that what I had mistaken for embarrassment was merely coldness. The policeman simply didn't care.

'Come on,' I said to George. 'I'll take you home.' I stood up and started to help him to his feet.

'Not that simple, I'm afraid, sir.' said the policeman.

I looked at him. 'What do you mean?'

'Your friend has been arrested, doctor.'

'Arrested? Why?'

'He hit one of the youths with his stick.'

'I'm not bloody surprised!'

'The youth has complained.'

'Was he injured?'

'The doctor says he'll have a bruise on his leg.'

'George is 84-years-old for God's sake! And they killed his dog!'

'The inspector says we could do him for carrying a dangerous weapon.'

'A walking stick! A dangerous weapon?'

The policeman shrugged. 'I'm just doing my job,' he said.

I lifted George to his feet. 'I'm taking him home,' I said firmly. 'He's my friend and so that's *my* job.'

For a moment I thought that the policeman was going to stop me. But he didn't. I took George back to Bilbury Grange and Patsy and I kept him with us for a week. He never recovered from the sorrow of losing Sally and he died two months later of a broken heart. I sometimes despair when I look at the type of people with whom we have to share this world of ours.

# VIETNAM VET

'Have you heard the news?' demanded Thumper, when I entered the Duck and Puddle last Wednesday lunchtime.

'Don't tell me Frank has been found sober?'

'No!' laughed Thumper. 'Nothing as spectacular as that.' He emptied his glass so that he would be able to take advantage of my unspoken but expected offer to buy him another drink.

'Go on...,' I sighed. 'Tell me!' I gestured to Frank to refill Thumper's glass and picked up the pint he'd pulled for me.

'We're going to have a celebrity visiting the village!'

'Who?'

'I don't know his name but he's a Vietnam Vet! He's touring Devon to promote some book he's written and the vicar has fixed up for him to come to Bilbury to speak to the Young Wives Group.'

'Pretty impressive,' I agreed. 'I once read that there are supposed to be hundreds of those guys living in the wilds because they can't get used to civilised life again.'

'I read about one who nearly killed his mother,' said Thumper. 'He was staying at home and she bent down to wake him up with a cup of tea. Before she could move he had her pinned to the wall with his forearm pressing into her throat.' He lifted his arm to demonstrate the move.

'Frightening!' I agreed, backing away. 'I'll be fascinated to see what this chap has got to say. Do you know if the Young Wives Group committee is allowing visitors?'

Thumper shrugged. 'I don't know. But Anne usually does the sandwiches so I'll have a word with her if you like.' Anne said that under the circumstances the committee had decided to make a break with tradition and to open up the meeting to anyone who wanted to go, and so last night Thumper and I joined the rest of the village in our local hall. The place was packed.

'I don't think we've had such a good turn out since we had that weather forecaster from the television,' said Gilly Parsons. She wrinkled up her nose. 'I can't remember his name now but he always used to wear those funny waistcoats.'

'Does anyone know this bloke's name?' asked Thumper.

'I still don't understand what an isobar is...,' muttered Gilly.

Anne shook her head. 'We got him on the vicar's recommendation,' she said. 'He heard about him through someone in Exeter.'

'I bet he's got some good tales to tell,' said Thumper, rubbing his hands together. 'Jumping out of helicopters and all that. Did you see that film?'

I tried in vain to remember the name of the film. 'I gather that most of those guys were hooked on drugs by the time they got home. I wonder if he had any problems like that?'

'They had a pretty good time in Saigon though!' said Thumper. 'Wall to wall women as I've heard it.'

He's probably more interested in the philosophical side of things,' said Gilly. 'I've heard that quite a lot of them have become very religious. That's probably why the vicar heard about him.'

Thumper looked disappointed. 'I hope he hasn't become totally boring,' he said, sounding rather worried. He looked around to plan his escape route but the hall was so crowded that escape was impossible. It was, in any case, too late for as he spoke the vicar walked out onto the stage.

'Ladies and gentlemen,' said the vicar, putting stress on the third word to emphasise what an unusual meeting this was, 'I'm delighted to see such a good turn out. I know you're all going to enjoy this evening's meeting and so without further ado I would like you to welcome our very special speaker...,' he waved an arm towards the side of the stage and a diminutive oriental walked briskly onto the stage, bowed and grinned at us all.

'Ladies and gentlemen, please give a big welcome to D'Ing Ling Dong - a veterinary surgeon who has come to talk to us about his experiences at the Saigon Missionary Hospital for Animals.' The vicar clapped his hands together enthusiastically.

There was a rather prolonged and embarrassing silence for a few moments, broken eventually by a smattering of polite applause. It wasn't quite the sort of Vietnamese vet that any of us had expected but even Thumper had to agree that under the Trades Descriptions Act none of us had any cause for complaint.

It was, I suppose, quite an interesting talk if you're interested in Vietnamese pot bellied pigs.

# THE COACH TRIP

The villagers of Bilbury are a hard-working lot. They do not feel entirely comfortable with holidays and they are not easily tempted away from their regular domestic and commercial duties.

The men in particular seem to take their responsibilities seriously. Unlike the men in cities, who seem constantly eager to abandon their homes and their jobs to follow football teams around the country, Bilburians can usually only be tempted from the village by an earnest and determined quest for knowledge and self-improvement.

When there are real prospects that the thirst for knowledge can be quenched the men of Bilbury will set aside their love of their village, temporarily abandon their fierce and selfless loyalty to their loved ones and sally forth into the outside world with all the vigour and courage of Crusaders setting off into the unknown. In Bilbury the good of a greater cause reigns for ever supreme over such trivial and insignificant forces as personal comfort, private pleasure and individual ambition.

During the summer, for example, Peter Marshall, shopkeeper, postman, undertaker and 24 hour dry cleaning agent, organised a coach trip to the Yeovil Show.

This adventure attracted an immediate and public-spirited response from two dozen men who were eager to demonstrate their willingness to sacrifice the joyful sense of self-satisfaction to be gained from a day spent quietly working so that the village might benefit from a supply of new ideas.

Encouraged by Thumper and Frank and carried along by this feeling of social responsibility I agreed to join the trip.

We set off early so that we could, as Kevin Montgomery explained, 'drink copious draughts from the well of knowledge in Yeovil' and so 'quench our thirst for useful information'.

'These trips are a vital part of village life,' Thumper told me. 'Information we obtain at the summer Shows helps us plan and make the best of our lives in the village.'

We were on the coach by 6.30 a.m., on the road by 6.40 a.m. and in Yeovil by 10 a.m.; our journey punctuated only by a ninety minute stop for essential fuel and lubrication.

(The high grease content fuel we bought from a lorry drivers' cafe and the lubrication we took from one of several crates which Peter, with foresight, had packed for what Frank described as 'social emergencies'. The coach, which had been adequately fuelled, in his absence, at Edwin Jackson's farm pump in order to minimise what Peter described as the 'nonessential' expenses of the journey, required no attention).

At the Yeovil Show Peter parked the coach in a field ('no point in paying car parking charges' explained Peter, 'we can use our money much more wisely than that') and we walked two miles across country before climbing over an eight foot high metal fence to get into the showground ('no point in paying entrance money,' said Thumper, 'it don't seem right for there to be a charge for knowledge').

All this exercise had made us sweat a little in the warm, morning, summer sunshine and I was by no means unenthusiastic when Frank suggested that we begin our day with a visit to the Beer Tent.

With pints of beer set before us Frank and Thumper then proceeded to plan our day, doing so with the precision of generals organising a military campaign.

When we had finished our beer we moved a few yards away into the hospitality tent of a large tractor manufacturer where pint glasses full of beer were thrust into our hands by girls dressed for some inexplicable reason in Bavarian costumes. Thumper and Kevin looked at a couple of tractors and stuffed a pile of brochures into their pockets.

Next, we visited the hospitality tent of a cattle feed supplier where girls dressed in brief shorts and T-shirts gave us pints of beer and small cubes of cheese on toothpicks.

From there we went onto the hospitality tent of a bank where tall girls dressed in dark grey suit jackets and tiny white shorts gave us glasses of sherry, stuffed olives and salty biscuits.

After taking a leisurely and restful lunch in the official Beer Tent we spent an exhausting afternoon visiting another series of hospitality tents.

We accepted glasses of cider from girls dressed in flimsy red skirts and diaphanous white blouses, glasses of lager from girls dressed in short kilts and tartan jumpers, and large glasses of white wine from girls dressed in French peasant costumes.

Afterwards we went back to the Beer Tent and had a meeting.

'How many votes for the Gamekeeper's Best Bitter?' asked Frank, licking the end of his pencil. He carefully counted the number of raised hands and then made a note on a folded tractor brochure. 'And how many for the Old Grey Beard Cider?' Again he made a careful note of the number of votes cast.

At seven sharp we set off for home, making an early start so as to make sure that we got back to the Duck and Puddle before closing time.

'I think we can regard that as a very educational and very successful day,' said Frank, speaking slowly, when we stopped briefly for light refreshments at a pub called the Ferret and Weasel in Little Witton.

I looked up at him and frowned. 'Educational?'

Frank pulled the tractor brochure out of his jacket pocket and showed it to me. 'There you are,' he said, pointing a podgy finger at some indecipherable scribble. 'We've got the names of three good draught beers and a cider that the Duck and Puddle has never stocked before.' He carefully refolded the brochure and put it away.

'Very informative day,' said Peter Marshall.

'I'll drink to that,' said Thumper, emptying his glass.

# A PHEASANT SURPRISE

David Faraday came into the Duck and Puddle yesterday evening looking as though he had just seen a ghost. I've seen snow which had a better colour.

'What on earth has happened to you?' asked Frank, pouring a large, medicinal brandy and pushing it across the counter.

David picked up the glass, knocked back the brandy and shuddered. Then he put the empty glass down, pushed it silently back across the counter to Frank and nodded. Frank quickly refilled the glass and David emptied it, just as quickly.

'I needed that,' he said.

We waited.

'I had to drive up to London this morning,' he began at last. 'Have you ever been on the road out near Simonsbath early in the morning?'

We all had and there was a general murmuring to that effect.

'I very nearly had a nasty accident before I'd really started,' he said. 'I'd forgotten just how dazzling the sun can be early in the morning,' he said. 'It's not so bad when you're driving due East on a straight road. You can get used to the rising sun when you know where it is. But that road twists and turns and one minute you can see perfectly well and the next moment you turn a corner and the damned sun blinds you completely.'

'I once put my truck into the ditch on that road,' confessed Thumper. He shook his head at the memory.

'I went round the corner by Jack Marshall's farm and suddenly couldn't see anything!' said David. 'I slammed my foot on the brake but before I could stop I felt a dull thud and heard a squawking and screeching from somewhere on the right. I got out and walked back. I was lucky not to have hit the side of Jack's barn. The fattest pheasant you'd ever seen was lying on the side of the road.'

'Nasty corner that,' said Frank, nodding wisely.

'It seemed like a good start to the day and there wasn't any point in leaving it there,' continued David. 'So I picked it up and threw it into the boot.'

Thumper, who has been known deliberately to collect pheasant out of season in this unorthodox fashion, nodded his approval.

'I went into London, did my bit of business and was on my way back home again when I found myself in a long queue to get onto the M4,' continued David. 'I tuned into the local radio station and found that the police were hunting for a couple of terrorists who had kidnapped a diplomat's wife in Kensington.'

'I hate London,' said Frank. He shivered. 'Horrible place.' There was a general murmuring of agreement with this observation and Frank refilled everyone's glasses so that we could drink a toast of damnation to our capital city.

'I'd just breathed a sigh of relief because I'd got to the front of the queue when suddenly this huge guy in a blue flack jacket, wearing a dark blue helmet with a plastic visor, thrust the business end of an automatic rifle in through the car window and screamed at me to keep my hands in view,' said David.

There were sharp intakes of breath all around the bar as we waited for David to carry on.

'What the hell did you do?' asked Frank.

'What do you think I did?' asked David. 'I did what I was told. The guy reached into the car, turned off the ignition and took my keys and then stepped back and told me to get out of the car very slowly keeping my hands in view all the time.'

Frank, who had emptied his own glass, poured himself another quadruple whisky in a vain attempt to stop his hands from shaking. I like Frank but I do not think he would be a good man to have alongside in an emergency.

'They said they'd heard a noise coming from my boot and before I could say or do anything two of them had searched me and pinned me to the side of a van while another three all aimed their rifles at the boot while a bloke with no helmet on reached out and used my key to open it.'

Frank took a huge gulp out of his whisky and leant forwards, waiting.

'Well, the boot lid lifted up and the pheasant flew out,' said David. 'It landed on the Cromwell Road for a moment, squawked a bit, flapped its wings and then took off over the traffic; flying, so one of the coppers told me, towards Regents Park.'

'Did they let you go then?' asked Frank.

'They searched my boot,' said David. 'But all they could find was an empty oil can, a pair of grubby gym shoes, a few tools and the spare tyre. So they told me I was lucky they hadn't charged me with wasting police time and let me go.'

'Phew!' said Frank. 'I'm glad I never go to London.'

'Did you get the pheasant back?' asked Thumper, who has a way of putting his finger on the crucial issues.

'No,' said David sadly. 'And the damned thing had crapped all over the carpet in my boot as well.'

'What a day,' said Frank. 'Have another brandy.'

'I don't mind if I do,' said David, wearily.

# AMERICANS IN BILBURY

Although it is situated right in the middle of one of the most beautiful parts of England, Bilbury is a little bit off the mainstream tourist track and we don't get as many visitors passing through as do nearby villages such as Lynton, Lynmouth and Clovelly.

So, when two Americans called Arlene and Homer Trout booked in at the Duck and Puddle for a week's holiday they caused quite a stir, especially since they let it be known that they were on a bit of a buying spree and were looking out for antiques to take back to their home in Texas.

Within twenty four hours of their arrival, local antique dealer Patchy Fogg had sold them a grandfather clock, a pine wall cupboard, a handmade pair of bellows that had been recovered from Camelot Castle and probably used by King Arthur himself, and a set of wooden bowls which had once been the property of Sir Francis Drake. Peter Marshall, the village shopkeeper, had persuaded them that a rusty old tree saw which has been lying amidst the rubbish behind his woodshed for years would look perfect hanging up over their fireplace.

Naturally, it wasn't long before Thumper Robinson turned up and I have to admit that it was a joy to watch him at work.

'Did I hear someone say that your name was Trout?' asked Thumper, after introducing himself to Arlene and Homer.

Arlene and Homer confirmed that he had heard correctly and that their name was, indeed, Trout.

'How remarkable!' said Thumper.

'Why is that remarkable?' asked Homer, who couldn't have responded better if he'd been coached.

'I don't suppose your family originally came from this part of the world, did they?' asked Thumper.

Arlene and Homer beamed. 'Well, we don't rightly know!' admitted Homer. 'But my grand-daddy always said that his forebears came over on the Mayflower.'

'Isn't that remarkable!' sighed Thumper.

'Do you know anyone around here with the name?' asked Arlene.

'Of course!' said Thumper. 'Old Granny Trout at Daffodil Cottage!'

Frank, the landlord, and I exchanged glances. Patchy who was standing nearby gazed on in admiration.

'Can we meet her?' asked Arlene, breathlessly.

'Well, I'll see if it's possible,' said Thumper. 'Give me a day or two.'

The following evening the Trouts were back in the pub. Thumper approached them with a broad grin on his face. 'I've spoken to old Granny Trout,' he told them. 'And she'd like to meet you. She says her father always used to talk about someone in the family having emigrated to the New World.'

Arlene and Homer held each other's hands and gazed at Thumper as though he'd just told them he could sell them the secret of eternal life for five dollars.

'I'll take you round there now, if you like,' offered Thumper, generously. 'It's only five minutes away in the car.'

The Trouts didn't need to be asked twice. Less than a minute later they were looking for the non-existent seat belts in Thumper's battered and beltless truck.

They were gone for around an hour and returned, without Thumper, looking as though they'd just seen the Holy Grail.

'How did you get on?' Frank asked them. They were clutching something which was crudely wrapped in old wallpaper.

'Wonderful!' said Arlene. 'Granny Trout is a marvellous old woman. Eighty-three and as bright as a button.'

'She's convinced we must be related,' said Homer. 'She says I'm the spitting image of her brother.'

'He died in the war,' Arlene explained, rather sadly.

'What's in the parcel?' asked Frank.

Homer carefully unfastened the wrapping paper. 'It's the old family bible!' he explained. He opened it and showed us two pages of faded, spidery writing at the front of the book. 'There you are!' he said. 'The Trout family history!'

'Granny Trout wanted us to have it,' said Arlene. 'Wasn't that wonderful of her?'

'Marvellous!' agreed Frank.

'She didn't sell it to you, I don't suppose?' I asked them.

'Good heavens, no!' said Arlene.

'So no money changed hands?' said Frank.

'Well, we asked Thumper if the old lady needed anything and he said her roof leaked,' said Arlene.

'So we've given him some travellers' cheques so that he can have her cottage re-roofed,' added Homer.

'That's very kind of you,' said Frank.

'It was the least we could do for her,' said Arlene. 'We're all she's got.'

That wasn't strictly true.

Most of us know Granny Trout at Daffodil Cottage rather better as Olive Robinson.

She's Thumper's aunt.

# THE FENCE

Living out in the country is wonderful but there are occasional disadvantages. For example, if you suddenly find you need something from the shops it can mean a round trip of twenty miles or more if Peter Marshall doesn't stock what you need at the village shop.

I usually try to plan my shopping so that I keep the number of journeys I need to make down to a minimum.

But it doesn't always work out as simply as I would like.

For example, take what happened at the end of last week when I decided that I wanted to plant a dozen small oak trees in a corner of the meadow behind the house. A recent gale had brought down a dozen oaks and I wanted to replace them as soon as possible.

I knew that if I didn't fence the area where I was going to put the young trees the sheep would strip the leaves and shoots from the saplings within minutes. Sheep may not be quite as destructive as goats but they do love the tender young shoots growing on shrubs, bushes and trees.

A local gardener told me that it would take a day's work to put up the fence and plant the trees. I felt sure I could do the job in less time and so I decided I'd do the job myself. Since the weather was decent enough last Saturday that was the day I decided to do it.

I needed a roll of stockproof fencing wire and a couple of dozen fence posts so I drove down to see Peter Marshall at the village shop in Bilbury. I just naturally assumed that he would sell such obviously agricultural items.

Peter's shop has the biggest range of goods on sale that I've ever seen anywhere. Most of the villagers are so accustomed to being able to find what they need there that they call *his* shop 'Harrods'. I once went into his shop clutching a shopping list which included: a handful of six inch masonry nails; two handfuls of two and a half inch vine eyes; twelve first class postage stamps; a packet of self-seal envelopes; a replacement handle for a garden fork; a pint of strawberry ice cream; a tin of dressmaking pins; a roll of cotton wool; two 150 watt light bulbs; a wholemeal loaf of bread; fourteen pounds of sugar and a bottle of malt whisky. I came away with everything I wanted wrapped in individual brown paper bags. And I had a choice of three different types of malt whisky.

But although Peter sells most things, he doesn't sell fencing stakes or wire and I came away disappointed and rather disillusioned; my faith in the village store slightly dented.

(I did not, of course, come away from Peter's shop entirely empty handed. It is, I firmly believe, quite impossible to come out of that shop without buying *something*. Unable to buy the stakes and fencing material that I needed I came away clutching a brown paper bag containing two cream doughnuts, another paper bag containing a pound of pears and a bicycle repair kit with which to mend my wellington boots.)

The result of my disappointment was that I had to drive into Barnstaple to buy what I needed.

Still, it didn't take too long and less than an hour after setting off I arrived back at Bilbury Grange with two dozen six foot high stakes and a roll of stock netting in the boot of the car.

After stopping at Bilbury Grange for a cup of tea and one of Peter Marshall's doughnuts, I backed the car down the lane towards the meadow and unloaded the stakes and fencing. It was then that I realised that I didn't have a large enough hammer to put the stakes into the ground. I immediately drove down to the village shop.

'I can let you have one of these,' said Peter, looking very glum and offering me a small lump hammer. 'But you really need a long-handled sledgehammer or the blunt side of a pick axe. I sold my last sledgehammer three weeks ago and I haven't restocked yet.'

I sensibly declined the lump hammer, bought a packet of drawing pins, two spare batteries for my torch, a packet of chocolate digestive biscuits and a pen refill and then drove back into Barnstaple.

Once again it took me less than an hour to get into Barnstaple and back.

When I got back to Bilbury with my sledgehammer and a patented wire cutting tool I popped into the house to have another cup of tea and a couple of chocolate digestive biscuits and then took the sledgehammer down to the meadow.

It was only after I had measured out a corner of the meadow, and hammered the fencing posts into the ground, that I realised that I didn't have any staples to hold the fencing onto the posts.

Peter was definitely embarrassed about not having the staples in stock.

'What can I say?' he said, miserably. 'Dr Brownlow bought up all my staples last Wednesday.'

I came away with a packet of marzipan, two dozen candles (ready for the next power cut), a packet of razor blades and a plastic rubber band dispenser. I then drove into Barnstaple for the third time that day.

This time there was more traffic and the first two ironmongers I tried had also sold out of staples. The result was that the journey there and back took me an hour and a half.

By the time I had finally stapled the wire to the posts I was exhausted and it was getting dark. I threw the tools and what was left of the wire netting and the staples into the boot of the car and drove home via the Duck and Puddle.

'You look pretty well knackered,' said Frank, handing me a pint without my having to say a word.

'Hard day,' I told him.

'What have you been doing?'

'Planting trees,' I said. 'Well, putting up a fence, actually,' I admitted. I sighed. 'I thought I'd save time and do it myself.'

The job had taken me a whole day and I hadn't even started to put any trees into the ground.

# THE BURNING HOUSE ON HOLLERDAY HILL

I don't like going to London. For one thing it's a long tedious journey. Even by train the journey is exhausting. It doesn't help that the trains are often dirty and overcrowded and the fact that they rarely seem to run on time just makes things even worse.

Apart from the fact that it takes several hours to get there, and that when you are there the dirt, the litter and the endless queues make life miserable and depressing, I dislike London because it always seems full of people who are so busy and full of their own sense of self-importance that they have no time for simple old-fashioned values such as courtesy.

I have, perhaps, grown too accustomed to the kinder, more sympathetic people who live in Devon in general and the gentle pace at which life moves in Bilbury in particular.

In London I always have the feeling that if I were to collapse in the street people would just step over me and carry on without any concern for my welfare. If anyone did bend down it would probably be to rob me rather than to help me.

When I had finished my meeting with a publisher in the centre of London I took a taxi to Paddington station and squeezed onto one of the early evening West Country trains. By the time we got to Reading it was running nearly half an hour late and by the time we arrived back in Taunton, where I had left my car, the train was the best part of an hour late.

Wearily, I climbed down off the train and walked the short distance from the railway station to the car park where I had left my car. It was a cool but clear evening and although the sun had long since set there was a full moon so visibility was good.

I always enjoy the drive back across Exmoor and along the coast towards Lynton. At night and out of the holiday season, there is rarely much traffic on the coast road and even after dark the views across the moors and the Bristol Channel are breathtaking. Between Porlock and Lynton you can see lights sparkling all along the Welsh coast. It was about nine o'clock, maybe a little later, when I drove around a bend five or six miles away from Lynton and saw that the whole of the sky above the village was bright red and orange with flames.

There was no doubt in my mind that there was a major fire in the village.

It was a terrifying sight and I increased my speed in order to get there as soon as possible.

As I drove I tried to keep my eye on the flames as much as I could. Occasionally, as the road twisted and turned, I lost sight of the fire and the orange sky, but, whenever I was in a position to see the hill above the village, the flames were clear and bright.

The road along the coast is narrow and hazardous at that point and even though I drove as quickly as I dared it still took me seven or eight minutes to cross the moors from the place where I had first seen the flames to the top of Countisbury Hill, where I could see the villages of Lynton and Lynmouth.

I slowed down as I reached the top of the hill, hoping that I could see where the fire was situated. I knew that it would take fire fighting crews and ambulances from Barnstaple at least half an hour to reach the town. There is a fire engine and an ambulance in Lynton but from the size of the blaze I felt sure that they would need help.

Strangely, from the top of Countisbury Hill, I could see nothing. No flames, no fire, no devastation - nothing. The flames had gone and the fire had disappeared. I was astonished and relieved.

I drove down across the bridge in Lynmouth, up the hill and along the A39 back to Bilbury.

The next morning, still puzzled, I drove back to Lynton and asked one of the shopkeepers if there had been any fires in the village the night before. The shopkeeper shook his head. There had been nothing that he knew of. Confused, I told him that I thought I had seen flames coming from the village. The source of the fire, I explained, seemed to me to have been some houses on the hill behind the village.

The shopkeeper nodded. 'Hollerday Hill,' he said. I looked at him, still not understanding.

'The big house on Hollerday Hill,' he went on. I waited.

'It burned down,' he finished.

'Is that the hill right behind the town?' I asked him. He nodded.

'It looked like a big blaze,' I said.

'It was a huge house. Massive country house. It burned to the ground.'

'Was anyone hurt?' I asked, anxiously.

The shopkeeper screwed up his eyes and thought for a few moments. 'I can't remember,' he said.

'But you must know!' I insisted. 'It must have been the biggest fire Lynton has ever had!'

'It was,' agreed the shopkeeper.

I couldn't understand why he seemed so unconcerned. 'Who lives there?' I demanded. 'You must know them!'

'Sir George Newnes lived there,' replied the shopkeeper. 'And my grandfather might have known him but I certainly never did. The house burnt down 50 years ago. It's been a wreck for half a century.' I stared at him.

The shopkeeper opened a drawer in a cabinet behind him and rummaged around for a few moments. Suddenly, triumphantly, he produced a booklet about the history of the village. He opened the booklet and flicked through the pages.

'Here you are!' he said. He showed me a picture of a burned out wreck of a house.

I looked at the date underneath the photograph.

When I had driven across the moors and seen the flames engulfing Lynton it had been exactly 50 years after the burning of the house on Hollerday Hill.

# MRS DUNCAN'S VISITORS

I first met Pearl Barley when I was practising as family doctor in Bilbury. Dr Brownlow was still the principal and I was his assistant.

'My real name is June but everyone calls me Pearl,' she said. She looked slightly older than the 65 her medical record card said she was. She wore a thick woollen coat and a small hat which had a rather sad looking bunch of artificial fruit sewn onto the brim. The colours of the cherries had faded to a dull and lifeless pink.

'Don't you want to take your coat off? I asked her.

She hesitated and then slowly unbuttoned her coat. When she had removed it she looked around before laying it gently on the examination couch. Underneath she wore a dark blue woollen skirt, a light blue nylon blouse and a full length flowered pinafore.

Mrs Barley looked shy, and stood almost at attention in front of the desk.

I pointed to a chair and smiled at her, trying to put her at her ease. 'How can I help you?'

'Could I have another prescription for some stockings for my veins?' she asked, sitting down. Timidly, she raised the hem of her skirt and showed me her elastic stockings. They were baggy, wrinkled and holed in several places.

'Are those your only pair?'

She nodded.

'But how on earth do you manage?'

The shyness slowly turned into embarrassment. 'I wash them every night and leave them in front of the fire to dry.' I reached for my prescription pad and then remembered that I had signed the last form for my previous patient. 'I'll just have to pop and get another pad of prescriptions from the receptionist.'

I was away no more than a minute or so and when I walked back into the room I had quite a shock. Mrs Barley had moved around to my side of the desk and was rummaging around in the drawers in my desk.

When she saw me Mrs Barley reddened and leapt back from the desk as though it had suddenly become red hot. She started to say something and then stopped.

Once I'd sat her down again and convinced her that I wasn't going to call the police I managed to persuade her to tell me what she had been looking for.

'Visiting cards,' she confessed at last.

I was so surprised that I nearly laughed.

'My visiting cards? But I don't have any.'

'It doesn't matter whose name is on them.'

It took another ten minutes to get the explanation.

'I work for Mrs Duncan. Do you know her?'

'I've heard of her.' Mrs Duncan was an elderly, rich and reclusive widow who lived in a large, detached house on the Barnstaple road. Dr Brownlow had told me that she had wanted to join his list as a private patient. When he had refused she had insisted on registering herself with a doctor in Barnstaple.

'She lives in the past a little. She's very grand. Her husband was in the diplomatic service.' Mrs Barley clearly had a great deal of respect for her employer. There was probably more than a little affection mixed in with it. 'She can be a bit, well, barbed.' She paused. 'But she's a real lady.' She put the emphasis very firmly on the word 'lady'.

'So why on earth do you need the visiting cards?' I asked her gently.

'She's very lonely. She hasn't got any family and her friends have all passed away. So no one ever comes to visit her. But she's very proud and she doesn't like to think that she never gets any visitors.'

'So you take in visiting cards?'

Mrs Barley nodded. 'And she tells me that she is busy and doesn't want any visitors.' She shrugged. 'It makes her feel better.'

'But what would you do if she said that she'd see them?'

Mrs Barley shook her head. 'I think she knows it's just a...,' she paused... 'well, just a sort of a game we play.'

I rummaged around in my desk and found some visiting cards. Half a dozen were from drug company representatives and one was from a double glazing company salesman. I handed the cards across the desk together with a prescription for three pairs of elastic stockings. Mrs Barley was overjoyed.

The next time I went into Barnstaple I called in at the printers and got them to give me a whole handful of sample visiting cards. I've put them in the drawer of my desk for the next time that Mrs Barley comes to the surgery.

# HUBERT SPRING

The truly eccentric are never aware of their eccentricity; they behave in what to the rest of us may appear to be an unusual way not because they derive any pleasure from shocking but because what they do is, to them, perfectly sensible and rational.

Consider, for example, the case of Hubert Spring, well known in our village for his lasting and largely inexplicable habit of spending exactly one hour every day sitting naked in the arms of a gnarled and rather uncomfortable looking old apple tree which stands at the bottom of his garden.

(When asked by a radio reporter to explain his apparently peculiar habit Hubert, who was at the time blue with cold and covered with a thin but noticeable layer of frost, answered that he was merely reminding his body of its general good fortune. 'How,' he asked, 'can you enjoy the good things in life unless you are regularly reminded of how unpleasant life can be?' Hubert's logic was regarded as unassailable in the village since he is unfailingly cheerful and enjoys consistent and excellent health.)

Hubert, who lives in a tiny cottage overlooking the Bilbury village green and whose unusual habit has startled and surprised many a summer visitor, spent the first thirty years of his life working for the post office but retired when he won a delightfully obscene amount of money in an Irish lottery.

Lots of people who win large sums of money stoically claim that their lives will not be changed by their good fortune but Hubert was not so unimaginative. After walking out of his job he gave large sums of money to each of his three daughters, April, May and June (April and June are as yet unmarried and are still known as the Spring sisters but May has married a boy called Geoffrey Summers and is said locally to have enjoyed a well deserved seasonal promotion) and told a reporter from the local evening paper that he intended to use the rest of the money to make sure that he grows the largest onions in the county and makes life as miserable as he can for the hunting fraternity.

It was, insisted Hubert, his intention to show that money does make a difference. Hubert loves gardening and animals and has spent almost equal parts of his life attempting to win a prize in one of the local vegetable shows and campaigning against the barbarism of hunting.

His vegetable growing efforts have brought him one fourth prize and a commended and his campaign against hunting has won him a suspended prison sentence, a broken collar bone and an honorary mention in the journal of the Hunt Saboteurs Association.

Hubert's financial good fortune came too late to enable him to win any vegetable growing awards in that year's vegetable shows but in good time to enable him to satisfy his second ambition.

Everyone was anxious to see what Hubert would do.

There was a rumour that he had decided to spend his money on buying up a huge tract of land which was for sale but I thought that was unlikely. The land was by no means essential to the hunt and it wasn't Hubert's style.

Another local rumour suggested that Hubert might be considering buying a motorbike and creating havoc by riding round and round the hunt. I didn't think that was very likely either. Hubert's eccentricities have always been envisioned on a much larger scale than that.

In the event no one guessed what Hubert was going to do and we were all surprised by his opening gambit for the hunting season.

His timing was absolutely perfect.

The hunt had met at Blackmoor Gate and dogs, horses and men in red coats were all milling around yapping and whinnying when suddenly these traditional hunting noises were swamped by the sound of an approaching helicopter. The clump of policemen who had turned up to deal with any threatened violence looked up anxiously but impotently.

Seconds later a crop spraying helicopter appeared overhead and began to drench the assembled multitude with a particularly pungent, clinging and unpleasant brand of aftershave.

Peering from the passenger side of the helicopter Hubert could be seen waving part of one hand at the huntsmen.

The hunt had to be abandoned, of course. None of the dogs could smell anything and every possible scent for miles around had been wiped out.

Hubert explained later that when he had seen the crop spraying helicopter advertised for hire he had realised it was a heaven scent opportunity

# HANS FROM ACROSS THE SEA

Bilbury had a visitor from abroad for most of last week and it was an educational experience for us all.

Hans came over from Germany where he works as an electrical engineer in a large factory which makes pop up toasters.

Although he is married he came alone as a representative of a small community which is looking for a village with which it can 'twin'. He has been staying with the vicar but he has spent much of his time in the Duck and Puddle talking to the regulars. Most of us have had the feeling that we have been undergoing some sort of screening procedure. I am, however, pleased to say that we are all confident that we have failed.

Although our German visitor speaks almost perfect English there are some aspects to our way of life which seem to puzzle him.

Last Sunday afternoon, for example, when Hans came into the pub for the first time and introduced himself to Frank Parsons behind the bar, Frank shook his hand and said 'Hello, how are you?' not for a moment expecting anything other than a perfunctory and superficial reply.

But Hans replied to Frank's query with precise and very Teutonic efficiency.

'I had a little headache last night,' he said. 'But I think that was probably a result of my flight. I would also blame my flight for the digestive upset I have experienced since my arrival in your country. I also suffer a little with my blood pressure and I have arthritis in my left knee.' He stopped for a moment, clearly making sure that he had not missed anything and then smiled. 'How are you?' he asked.

'Fine, thanks.' replied Frank, with typically British understatement. Frank is overweight and has a liver the size of Cornwall; he suffers from chronic bronchitis, persistent high blood pressure and can't walk for more than five yards without having to sit down and rest.

'My village is looking for a twin,' said Hans.

'That's nice.' said Frank. 'Is your village like Bilbury?'

'No.' said Hans, visibly growing in stature as he told us about his home town. 'It is much, much bigger. We have twenty thousand inhabitants, four factories, an industrial estate, an Olympic size swimming pool and many, many four lane highways. Our football club won second place in our local league last year.'

'That's very nice.' said Frank, pouring Thumper a drink.

'Bilbury has a pond, a village green, one lane that takes two way traffic, a series of single track roads and a darts team that has come bottom in our local league for the last five years,' said Thumper, exaggerating somewhat. The darts team has, in fact, only come bottom of the league for four out of the last five years. Last year the Bilbury team came second from bottom and the celebrations in the Duck and Puddle lasted for nearly a week.

'What does your town want out of a twin?' asked Frank.

'We would like very much to enjoy a cultural and artistic exchange,' replied Hans. 'And to establish an exchange of business ideas.'

'I'm not sure that Bilbury is exactly the right place for you,' said Frank. 'We don't have much business going on here.'

'Unless you count insurance fraud,' I muttered under my breath.

'Our town has many powerful links and great industrial traditions,' said Hans. 'Your little village could learn a lot from an association with us. You could quickly expand and become big and prosperous like us.'

Peter Marshall, our local taxi driver, shop keeper, funeral service operator, 24 hour dry cleaning agent and part-time postman, sat up and began to look interested.

'We have a powerful system of local government,' said Hans. 'Through our taxes we use our wealth for the good of our community.'

Peter's interest evaporated.

'I don't think we're really all that keen on becoming big and prosperous,' said Thumper. 'We rather like life the way it is.'

'I'd better move,' I said, looking at my watch, suddenly remembering that I'd promised to be back home for dinner.

'What is the time?' asked Hans.

'Quarter to six.'

Hans looked very worried. 'I must go and change my shoes!' he announced.

We all looked at him.

'I have brown shoes on,' said Hans. He smiled proudly. 'I have read a book on how to behave in England. 'It says that after 6 p.m.

gentlemen always wear black shoes.' He slid off his bar stool, said goodbye to us all and left rapidly for his bedroom.

'I'm just glad I've got black wellington boots on,' said Thumper as Hans disappeared. He held out a leg so that we could admire his taste in footwear.

Most of us feel confident that Bilbury will not be getting twinned with any foreign towns. I'm afraid that none of us really feels that we are up to it.

# ENID AND ELSIE BYGRAVES

Enid and Elsie Bygraves are twins.

No one seems to know exactly how old they are but Gilly Parsons reckons they must be at least 85. They are both rather forgetful and they never hurry anywhere but they are fit and strong and eminent testimony to the virtues of simple, healthy living. They are as alike as two peas although if you get close enough you can tell them apart if you look for the freckle just in front of a right ear. If the freckle is there then you are looking at Enid. If it isn't then you are looking at Elsie.

(Or is it the other way around?)

Elsie and Enid have spent their entire lives together and they are still living in the same small cottage that they were brought up in at the beginning of the century. They had electricity installed in the 1960s but apart from that there have been few, if any, other changes to their home.

Seven weeks ago there was a considerable amount of anger in the village when the pair reported that their car, an ancient but reliable Ford Popular with just 17,000 miles on the clock, had been stolen from the garage at the side of their cottage.

No one could understand why car thieves would want to steal an old Ford Popular. Even though it had never been driven at more than 30 mph it didn't exactly have classic car status. And P.C.Wren, our local constable, confirmed that no joy rider would be seen dead in such a vehicle.

Elsie, who always drove (although Enid also had a driving licence) said that she had absolutely no idea when the car had been stolen. She told the police that she only ever opened the garage doors once a week when she went to get the car out for their weekly shopping trip.

The anger and outrage in the village was intensified by the knowledge that for Bilbury, crime had previously always been something we had read about rather than experienced. Most of us regularly leave our homes and cars unlocked and it was disturbing to think that our peace and trust had been so cruelly violated.

The police put the car on their missing vehicles list and with P.C. Wren's help Elsie and Enid filled in an insurance claim form.

Last week they received a cheque from the insurance company and in a mood of great excitement they went into Barnstaple in Peter Marshall's taxi and bought themselves a replacement; a good-looking, two door Ford Escort with twin exhausts, twin spotlights, fake fur seat covers and a pair of fluffy dice hanging in the back window. They were, they professed, very pleased with it. Elsie was particularly taken with the leatherette steering wheel which, she said, she liked a lot.

There has, however, been an unusual twist to Bilbury's first major crime story in years.

Enid and Elsie do not have a telephone in their cottage and yesterday evening Frank Parsons took a call at the pub from a man working at a garage in Barnstaple.

'Do you know a couple of old dears called Bygraves?' asked the caller.

Frank said that he did, indeed, know Enid and Elsie Bygraves.

'Are they O.K? They haven't died have they?'

'They're fine. Why?'

'Would you ask them if they'd like to come and collect their car?' asked the caller. 'It has been cluttering up my garage for weeks now.'

'I don't understand,' said Frank, who didn't understand.

'They brought it in for a service but they've never come back to pick it up. If they don't pick it up soon we'll have to sell it to pay the bill.'

Frank said he'd try to get in touch with the sisters and asked the garage man not to do anything hasty.

'What do we do?' Frank asked Thumper Robinson and me.

'They must have taken the Ford Popular over to Barnstaple, left it for a service, got a taxi back home and then completely forgotten about it! If they go and pick it up the insurance company isn't going to be very pleased.'

I looked at Thumper and waited. He is our local expert on insurance matters.

Thumper sipped at his beer and shook his head sagely. 'I'll sort it out,' he promised. He looked at me. 'But I'm not going to tell *you* what I'm going to do. I don't want the insurance company reading about it in one of those books of yours.'

# THE ARTIST

Ian's parents were wealthy enough to send him to private school and ambitious enough for him to want him to have a good career in one of the professions. At their insistence he applied for and won a place to study law at university.

But he gave it all up three months before he was due to qualify, bravely telling his horrified parents that he could not contemplate spending his life making people miserable. There was, he insisted, no link between justice and the law and he was not prepared to spend his life taking advantage of people's fears, anxieties, shortcomings and weaknesses.

After spending a month on holiday in Europe, Ian returned home to find that his parents had fixed him up with a job as a life insurance salesman.

'If you won't make a career in law,' said his father firmly, 'then you'll have to have a career in business.'

Ian began his business career by failing as a life insurance salesman. He was far too honest for his own good and no one ever bought any policies from him.

He went on to fail as a double glazing salesman, an encyclopaedia salesman and an estate agent. He did not enjoy any of these jobs and (Ian readily admits) was not very good at them either.

For a while Ian worked as an assistant manager in a supermarket. But he left there after a row about the way the check-out girls were treated.

By the time he was 35 Ian had failed at just about every job known to man. His parents, who'd had such high hopes for their son, told him that they washed their hands of him.

For one whole summer Ian wandered rather aimlessly around the coast of Devon and finally settled in Bilbury where he rented a small, tumbledown cottage and planned to earn a modest living doing whatever odd jobs he could find.

In the summer he sold ice cream, helped out in the restaurants and cut lawns and in the winter he sold firewood.

Somewhere along the line (he had long since forgotten what had triggered his interest) Ian had acquired an enthusiasm for ornithology and with no steady job to interfere with his life he began to spend more and more of his time exploring the moors and cliff tops of the west country drawing and painting birds.

He had a natural, untutored talent for art and he had taught himself to identify a bird on the wing so well that even Thumper Robinson envied him this skill.

Occasionally he would sell one of his paintings though, to be honest, most of the sales were made to people who were more interested in helping him through a difficult patch than in collecting art. He was a very likeable fellow.

Apart from the dog with whom he shared his cottage, Ian had no responsibilities and no ties and no ambitions. He had very few possessions and approached each day with an innocent freshness that almost guaranteed happiness. Disappointments and setbacks were always regarded as temporary and of no real significance.

But six months ago something terrible happened to him.

A stranger turned up at the Duck and Puddle, driving a BMW and wearing a tweed hacking jacket, a pair of tweed plus twos and a deerstalker hat.

He was, he said, an art dealer from London. A friend had bought one of Ian's paintings while in Devon on holiday and the dealer told Ian he wanted to represent him and make him rich. There was, insisted the dealer, a heavy demand for the sort of old-fashioned painting that Ian produced.

At first Ian was reluctant even to see the dealer. But the man from London was very insistent.

Eventually, Ian signed a contract and the dealer handed over a cheque (which Ian, who did not have a bank account, had to cash at the pub) and went away with a car boot full of paintings.

Two months later the first journalists appeared. Then a television crew from an Arts programme (with a capital A).

Ian's life has now changed completely. He has, unwillingly, become a major celebrity in the art world. His pictures are being collected by the wealthy.

Ian is no longer the contented man he was. He is nervous and anxious and for the first time in years he cannot sleep.

The final irony in this story is that two days ago Ian's parents turned up to see him. They were, they said, very proud of him.

# THELMA AND JACQUI

When I was a family doctor I always kept a box of paper handkerchiefs on top of my desk in the certain knowledge that at every surgery there would be a few tears shed.

I remember one late September surgery when I started the evening with a half full box of tissues and ended it with nothing but an empty box.

First, there was Thelma Pettigrew.

Thelma, her husband and their three small children lived in a two bedroom cottage out on the edge of the moors. They had a two acre garden on which they grew most of their own food and they enjoyed one of the most spectacular views on Exmoor. Their cottage had no mains electricity and so the Pettigrews relied entirely on a small petrol driven generator which was constantly breaking down. They did all their cooking and got all their heat and hot water from a small wood burning stove in the kitchen.

'I think I need a bit of a tonic,' said Mrs Pettigrew. 'I feel really miserable.' Her eyes were red and she had clearly been crying. She wore a pair of faded jeans and a thick, home knitted jumper that looked as if it had probably been made for someone at least four sizes larger.

I asked her if there was anything in particular making her feel miserable.

She shrugged. 'Just life in general,' she said, wearily. 'I get up every morning and have to spend at least two hours trying to relight the stove.' She sighed. 'It always goes out during the night.'

There was a pause while she rummaged around in her pocket for a paper handkerchief. 'I hate that stove!' she said emphatically. 'And I'm sure it hates me.' She blew her nose noisily.

'As soon as I've got the stove alight I have to start the lunch, then there's the cooking and the washing and the ironing and as soon as I've done that I have to get out into the garden and weed the vegetable patch.' She twisted her handkerchief around and around in her fingers until it tore. I pushed my box of tissues across the desk towards her. She took one and blew her nose again.

'I spent three years at college and I've got a degree in Spanish,' she told me, the tears rolling down her cheeks. 'I should have studied stove lighting and nappy washing.' She took another tissue and wiped her eyes. 'There's no challenge in my life at all. I want more excitement, more action. I want something more demanding than lighting that damned stove.'

She stayed for nearly half an hour and my box of tissues was a lot emptier by the time she'd gone.

The patient who followed Thelma Pettigrew was someone I had never seen before.

'I don't suppose you can help me,' she said, even before she'd sat down. 'But I thought I'd call in on the off chance.'

She told me that her name was Jacqui (with a q) Tavistock and that she was on holiday, staying at a small boarding house on the Combe Martin road. She wore a black tracksuit with an emblem I didn't recognise emblazoned on the chest and had a pair of designer sunglasses pushed high up into her hair.

'I love it down here,' she sighed, and clearly meant it. 'I live in London and work for an advertising agency. I hate it there. There's never any time to think. Everyone is always rushing and everything is done in a panic.'

She said at first that she wanted to know if I could give her something to calm her down and help her relax but quickly confessed that what she really wanted was a sick note to send to her boss.

'I just can't cope with the idea of going back to that mad house,' she told me, with tears beginning to appear. She sighed and sniffed and I handed her the box of tissues. 'I do wish I could find a little cottage down here,' she said, dreamily. 'I'd love somewhere miles from anywhere. I could grow my own vegetables and do my own cooking and be independent. It would be wonderful.'

She had a ten tissue story to tell and I listened to her for twenty minutes before confessing that there really wasn't anything useful I could do, apart from give her the sick note she wanted so that she could steal another week's holiday.

When she'd gone I couldn't help thinking how strange life is and how wonderful it would have been if I had been able to help Thelma and Jacqui swop lives for a week or so.

But I couldn't help wondering just how long they would be happy living each other's lives.

# FISH PIE

Gilbert Halliwell had made his fortune as a builder in Wolverhampton and at the age of 55 had retired and bought a large and rather absurdly expensively converted barn on the outskirts of Bilbury. He bought himself a Range Rover, a brand new Barbour coat, a shooting stick and a hip flask.

Together with Maude, his wife, and Cynthia, his unmarried eldest daughter, Gilbert Halliwell wasted no time in doing what he could to establish himself as a stalwart of the local community. Within a year of coming to live in the village he had managed to get himself onto the Kentisbury Golf Club committee, had joined the nearest hunt, had made a generous donation to the church funds and had narrowly missed being elected onto the local Parish Council.

Gilbert desperately wanted to be a country gentleman.

He wanted local farm workers to touch their caps, nod slightly and say 'Good morning, Mr Halliwell, sir,' when he went past. He had been brought up in a terraced house in Wolverhampton and he now wanted everyone in Bilbury to treat him as a man of property.

Gilbert had just under an acre of garden and even he realised that this wasn't enough land to raise deer, breed exotic varieties of sheep or play host to the hunt.

And so he hired an expensive firm of landscape gardeners to throw money and muscle power at a fairly flat and rather ordinary piece of pasture land.

At the end of six months (and after handing over a cheque for a small fortune) Gilbert was the extremely proud owner of sixteen varieties of apple tree, a rose garden, a small kitchen garden, a Japanese garden and a pond.

He was particularly proud of the pond and of the five huge and very expensive coy carp which the landscape gardener had insisted were far more fashionable than goldfish or trout. Gilbert was 'sold' on them when he was told that all the really rich country folk had them in their lakes. At £6,000 each they were certainly the most expensive fish Gilbert had ever bought.

Sadly for Gilbert life was not as full of joy as he had hoped it would be. He was not an insensitive man and he was constantly aware of the fact that however hard he tried people were always sniggering about him behind his back.

Even worse was the fact that his wife was not happy in Bilbury. She missed the bright lights and shops of Wolverhampton and she desperately missed her friends and her twice weekly coffee mornings. She found Bilbury a rather lonely place and she hated the mud and the quiet of the country.

A few weeks ago Gilbert decided that in order to try to increase his local standing and to decrease his wife's sense of isolation he would hold a large dinner party in a marquee in his garden.

Maude, who was given the task of organising the affair and supervising the preparation of the meal, was not at all enthusiastic. In fact, she hated the whole idea.

But Gilbert insisted. He wanted the rest of Bilbury to experience some of the sophisticated style of Wolverhampton social life. In particular, he wanted Maude to make sure that the vegetables were taken from their own garden. 'I might not be able to serve my own venison!' he said. 'But I can serve my own potatoes!'

The dinner was held last Sunday. Together with most of the population of Bilbury I was there. And it was probably the most embarrassing evening of my life.

The big explosion took place when the main course was served.

'What's this?' demanded Gilbert, shouting to his wife across the marquee. 'I said I wanted beef!'

'It's fish stew,' replied Maude.

'I can see that!'

'Well, why did you ask me what it was then?'

'Because it isn't beef!' Gilbert lowered his nose and sniffed.

'What sort of fish is it?' he demanded.

'Home-grown,' answered Maude. 'Like the vegetables.'

It took a moment or two for Gilbert to realise what Maude meant.

Then he got very cross and said things that we all felt he would regret the following day. Together with the other guests I muttered something about suddenly remembering another engagement and left.

'Pity,' said Thumper. 'I've never eaten coy carp. Often wondered what the things taste like.'

I understand that Gilbert has now put his house on the market and is planning to return to Wolverhampton.

# WHEN MIDGES BITE

'I read a report in the paper this morning,' said Lionel Francis, 'that claimed that when a midge bites you it drinks one tenth of a millionth of a litre of blood.'

Lionel is the nearest thing we've got to an executive in Bilbury. He always wears a matching handkerchief and tie set and his two tone Ford car is equipped with twin halogen spotlights and a telephone.

The telephone doesn't work very well around Bilbury because the hills interfere with the reception but even a non-functioning telephone is something of a status symbol in a village where the grapevine is still the preferred method of message carrying.

Lionel, who runs a small chain of chemists' shops, doesn't often come into the Duck and Puddle because, as he once put it, he regards it as rather too 'rural' for his taste. (I think what he means is that too many of the customers come in wearing dung encrusted wellington boots).

'You can spare that much,' said Thumper.

This was a slightly barbed comment for Lionel, who has the reputation of eating for two, has the body to confirm the reputation. Peter Marshall still claims that it was Lionel Francis who broke the springs in his taxi.

'You may scoff!' admonished Lionel. 'But the report also stated that there are ten million midges to the acre on moorland.'

'This sounds like the beginning of one of those "If a man leaves the bath tap running how long will it take two boys with wheelbarrows to move six tons of sand to Llandudno" questions.' said Thumper. 'I could never do those at school.'

I started scribbling on a beermat. 'Did it say how many times a midge is likely to bite in an hour?'

'No.'

'Twice?'

'That sounds fair.'

'That means that the midges on one acre of moorland will drink two litres of blood an hour!' I announced. I did the sum again and found, to my surprise, that either the first answer was correct or else I had made the same mistake twice. In view of the fact that it was very nearly official closing time I thought that this was rather impressive.

(At official closing time Frank shuts the pub front door and doesn't let anyone else in. But he doesn't throw anyone out. For thirty years he has worked on the assumption that this is what the authorities mean by 'closing time' and since after 6 pm the local police stations all seem to be manned by telephone answering machines it seems unlikely that he will be forced to think otherwise.)

'How many litres of blood in the average human body?' Thumper asked me.

'Eight pints or so. What's that in litres?'

'Five.' answered Lionel instantly.

'So the midges on five acres of moorland will completely exsanguinate two human beings every hour.' I said, impressing myself again.

'Ex- what?' asked Thumper.

'Exsanguinate - completely empty all the blood out. Like vampires.'

Thumper put his glass down so heavily that some beer splashed out onto the bar counter. He immediately picked up a towel and started to mop up the mess he'd made. A stranger might have been impressed by this apparently selfless act. 'The moors must be solid with dead bodies during the summer. You'd think we'd be falling over them!' He shivered. 'How many acres of moorland are there on Exmoor and Dartmoor?' Frank pulled a tourist guide down from a shelf behind the bar and rapidly thumbed through it. 'Exmoor is 265 square miles and Dartmoor is 365 square miles.'

'How many acres is that?'

'A lot.'

For a moment there was silence.

'Maybe the bodies all get eaten by maggots.' said Thumper, who was wringing out the towel over his beer glass. 'How many maggots are there to the acre, Lionel?'

Lionel frowned. 'I don't know. The article didn't say.'

'If I were you,' said Frank quietly, 'I'd stop reading those darned newspapers. If you hadn't read that stuff about midges none of us would be worried about this.' He shivered involuntarily. 'I'll tell you this for nothing – I shall keep my car windows shut next time I drive across the moors.'

'I reckon the police probably get someone to move all the dead bodies so that there isn't any public panic.' said Thumper, who, whenever there is any doubt, always believes in giving the conspiracy theory the benefit of the doubt. 'Either that or the Tourist Board have it done.'

'That's a lot of coffins and a lot of funerals,' said Peter Marshall from the village shop. We had all assumed he was fast asleep. 'I wonder if I could get the contract?'

# MRS LOVELACE'S MATCHBOX

An unholy row has broken out in Bilbury this week.

It started, as these things often do, with something very trivial: a competition at the monthly meeting of the Bilbury Women's Institute.

Organised by Mrs Parsons, the aim of the competition was to see how many small items could be crammed into a matchbox.

Last year Mrs Jellicoe's prize-winning matchbox contained twenty seven items (including a collar stud that, according to Mrs Jellicoe, once belonged to Lloyd George).

This year Mrs Lovelace, who lives in the main part of the Old Priory and whose most notable physical feature is an artificially enhanced pneumatic bust of unlikely proportions, won the competition easily with a matchbox that contained 559 ordinary steel sewing pins.

Not all the other members of the W.I. were happy about it.

'That's cheating!' insisted Mrs Bridgford, who never pulls her punches and who, with a matchbox crammed tightly with 31 different items, considered herself to the rightful winner of the competition.

(It is worth pointing out that Mrs Bridgford has never forgiven Mrs Lovelace for winning the Best Cake Prize at the Blackmoor Gate Show last summer. Mrs Bridgford has made no secret of the fact that she believes that the triple layered sponge that took Mrs Lovelace to victory was baked not by Mrs Lovelace herself but by her daily help - Mrs Pettigrew – a woman whose way with a sponge cake has long been legendary in W.I. circles.)

Mrs Lovelace rose to the bait like a trout to a May fly. 'How dare you!' she demanded, her hackles well and truly risen.

'Pins! Pins! Pins!' spat Mrs Bridgford. 'Anyone could have filled a matchbox with pins!'

'Just because you didn't think of it!' spat back Mrs Lovelace.

'I'm surprised you didn't get one of those huge, joke matchboxes,' said Mrs Bridgford. 'You could have got millions of pins in one of those.'

'That would have been against the rules,' Mrs Lovelace pointed out. She took a crumpled piece of paper out of her handbag, lay it out on her lap and straightened it. She took out her blue framed spectacles and put them on.

'Look!' she said, reading from the paper and pointing to the words as she pronounced them. 'Matchboxes must be no larger than two and a half inches long and one and a half inches wide.' She refolded the paper, put it back into her handbag, sat back, folded her arms and looked around the room defiantly.

But Mrs Bridgford was not about to give in so easily.

'It's still cheating!' she insisted. 'It's still against the spirit of the competition!'

And so it went on.

Mrs Lovelace repeated her assertion that Mrs Bridgford only objected because she hadn't thought of it, and Mrs Bridgford said that no one with an ounce of honesty would have thought of such a thing and Mrs Lovelace asked Mrs Bridgford if she was calling her dishonest and Mrs Bridgford said she was and that was when things really started to get out of control.

Mrs Parsons stood up and in a very loud voice asked if anyone wanted another cup of tea but no one took any notice of her at all.

Mrs Lovelace said that Mrs Bridgford smelt of silage and Mrs Bridgford said that at least she could sit by the fire without worrying that her silicone implants might melt, and after a moment's deafening silence Mrs Lovelace burst into tears and rushed out of the village hall and hurried home to tell her husband and he immediately went out and built a dam across the stream that leads down to the Bridgford farm.

And the upshot of *that* was that late last night, after dark, Albert Bridgford went up to the Lovelace's place with his double-barrelled shotgun under his arm and took a pick axe to the dam.

To complete the story I should tell you that the prize Mrs Lovelace won was a jar of home-made rhubarb jam which, in all the excitement, she forgot to take home with her. It is still standing on the village hall window sill waiting to be collected.

The jam was made by Mrs Norton and is widely reputed to need more sugar in it.

# THE JAZZ WEEKEND

When I first moved to North Devon I thought I might buy a boat and take up sailing.

When I mentioned this to Frank in the Duck and Puddle he suggested that I should telephone the local harbour master in the nearest coastal village.

'Have you got any spare moorings?' I asked Alf, the harbour master. Alf is not a full-time harbour master. He runs a petrol station for a living and works as harbour master for the power and the glory.

'How big is your boat?'

'I haven't bought one yet. I wanted to make sure that I could get a mooring first.'

'I can't give you a mooring until I know how big your boat is.'

The logic of this seemed solid and unassailable so I thanked the harbour master and put down the telephone. Later that evening, in the Duck and Puddle, I asked Thumper if he knew of any boats for sale.

'How big is your mooring?' Thumper wanted to know.

'I haven't got one yet.' I told him. 'I thought I'd buy the boat first and then get a mooring to fit it.'

Thumper sucked in air through clenched teeth and shook his head. Instinctively, I knew that something was worrying him.

'What's up?' I asked.

'Dangerous move!' he told me sternly. 'You could end up with a boat and no mooring. Then where would you be?'

His logic seemed equally unassailable. A boat without a mooring is like a bridge without a road.

'Get the harbour master to give you a mooring and then go out and buy a boat to fit it,' suggested Thumper.

'But what if I can't find a boat to fit my mooring?' I asked him, conscious that a mooring without a boat wasn't likely to be much fun.

That was eight years ago. I still haven't got a boat or a mooring.

\*\*\*

At first I thought that the fact that things did not change very rapidly in Bilbury was a result of a deliberate objection to progress, a reactionary attitude orchestrated by local politicians and sustained by a population which is wedded to tradition.

But, over the years, I have gradually come to realise that Bilbury remains firmly entrenched in the past not as a result of any deliberate, consciously thought out policy but as a result of its inhabitants' skilful ability to avoid making decisions of any kind. The people of Bilbury have turned procrastination into a sophisticated science. It is this, rather than any objection to change, which protects the village from any serious flirtation with the twentieth century. Bilbury folk have a powerful talent for repelling change without confronting it.

Some people would probably find all this rather tiresome. But I have long since stopped feeling frustrated. These days I rather like the Bilbury way of doing things. There is something very comforting about living in an unchanging world. After all, anything which results in change is also likely to lead to heartache, dissatisfaction and despair, whereas an absence of change means stability and reliability.

***

Bilbury's rather special variety of local logic can be very infectious. Today, I realised that I have become a true Bilburian. Without even thinking about it I have helped to preserve the status quo.

I walked into the Duck and Puddle at lunchtime to discover that Gilly, the landlady, had announced that she wanted to organise a Jazz Weekend in the village hall, bringing in bands from as far away as Bude and South Molton. Thumper, who could see his quiet weekend drinking haunt filling up with men in beards and corduroy trousers, was vociferously opposed to this proposal.

'Bilbury needs livening up a bit!' said Gilly, firmly.

'It will certainly do that!' agreed Frank loyally, though one could see that his heart wasn't really in it. Frank is at his happiest when he is pulling pints and drinking them himself. I knew that he wouldn't be keen on any increase in business if it meant spending his time pulling pints for other people to drink. Thumper took a large swig out of his beer, wiped froth off his mouth with the back of his hand and snorted.

I found myself firmly on Thumper's side.

I had no objection to the idea of listening to jazz for a weekend but I strongly suspected Gilly would want to put up advertisements and that as a result there would be strangers coming into the village.

*Strangers!*

'There is a snag,' I pointed out.

They all turned and looked at me.

'Don't you agree that this sort of thing only really works when it's a tradition?'

Even Gilly nodded.

'But it's never been done before here.'

'No,' agreed Gilly cautiously.

'So it isn't a tradition,' I pointed out.

'And so it's bound to be a failure.' nodded Frank, gloomily.

'We don't want Bilbury to be associated with a failure!' said Thumper firmly.

'Besides,' I pointed out, 'the village hall is always shut at weekends.'

The jazz festival has now been abandoned.

# AN UNROMANTIC MAN'S LAST ROMANTIC GESTURE

Keith Littlejohn did not live in Bilbury, nor, indeed, in Devon. He lived in a small town in Somerset, just over the county border. But he has truly earned his place in the history of the area for he came to Devon to commit suicide and he died not far from Bilbury, at the bottom of the tallest sea cliffs in England. For nine months Keith, a 22-year-old assistant supermarket manager, had been courting Lesley, a 21-year-old bank clerk. I know that the word 'courting' sounds old-fashioned but they were, in truth, an old-fashioned couple.

Keith sported a small, neatly-trimmed toothbrush moustache, had his hair cut in the old-fashioned, short back and sides 'pudding basin' style and, when not working, invariably wore a sports coat and grey flannels. He wore a trainspotter's enamel badge on his jacket lapel and carried a neat row of coloured pens in his breast pocket.

Lesley who was two inches shorter, wore her light brown hair in a neat, page-boy style and liked pleated skirts, fluffy jumpers and cameo brooches.

On warm, dry days they would drive to Lynmouth and spend the day walking along the cliff tops near Countisbury. On Saturdays they would share a pizza, go to the cinema and hold hands while walking back to the car park where Keith's neat and well-kept Vauxhall was waiting for them. Although at the end of the evening they would kiss each other, theirs was not what you could call a *physical* relationship.

Last Saturday Keith proposed to Lesley. It wasn't a particularly romantic moment. He didn't get down on his knees and he had not been presumptuous enough to purchase a ring. His precise words were: 'Shall we get married then?'

'Could I have 48 hours to think about it?' Lesley had asked, to Keith's surprise. 'It's not that I'm not sure,' she reassured him, though to be truthful that was exactly the problem. In recent months, Lesley had begun to suspect that she might be more of a romantic than she had ever previously realised.

'Of course!' Keith had replied, rather taken aback. He had rather assumed that they were stepping out together in the quiet, unspoken, expectation of matrimony.

'It's not you I'm not sure about it,' she had told him. 'It's just that I'm not sure that *I'm* ready to get married yet.'

'When will you know?' asked Keith.

'By Monday,' promised Lesley.

And so Keith took Lesley home, kissed her affectionately on the cheek and said he looked forward very much to hearing from her.

He heard nothing on Sunday and by 8 a.m. on Monday morning he was in deep despair. Lesley had promised to let him know by Monday and now it was Monday and he had heard nothing. Keith was convinced that this meant not only that Lesley was not going to marry him but also that she was not even going to reply. He felt disappointed, humiliated, let down and deeply depressed.

He climbed into his Vauxhall and instead of driving off to the supermarket he drove towards Lynmouth.

On the steep cliff road down from Countisbury he stopped his car for a few moments, and gazed out towards the Bristol Channel. Then he revved up the engine, bounced the car over the low grassy bank that was the only barrier which protected the road from a drop of several hundred feet down into the sea and slammed his foot down onto the accelerator.

The coroner told the young man's relatives that Keith died the instant his car hit the rocks below. The petrol tank had exploded with the impact and even if Keith had, by some miracle, survived the crash he could not have lived on through the inferno which followed. The irony in this tragedy is that Lesley had decided to accept Keith's proposal of marriage but in a moment of premeditated romanticism had telephoned the disc jockey at a local radio station and asked him to announce her acceptance during his programme. She knew that the supermarket where Keith worked normally carried the broadcasts from the radio station on its loud speaker system.

And the tragedy in the irony is that Keith's radio was tuned to the radio station Lesley had contacted. The local police technician who examined the car told me that judging by the time shown on the clock on the dashboard of Keith's Vauxhall the assistant supermarket manager had probably heard of his fiancée's acceptance of his proposal just as his car plummeted over the cliff edge.

.

# THE TEMPORARY RESIDENT

I had many strange experiences when I was a family doctor. When you press the buzzer underneath your desk you never know who is going to come in next or what story they will tell.

One evening, after a long and at times seemingly never ending day, I stood up and started to stuff my stethoscope into my jacket pocket, thinking I had seen my last patient. Suddenly, and unexpectedly, Miss Johnson, the receptionist, poked her head round the door.

'There's one more patient waiting for you, doctor,' she said 'He came just as I was shutting the front door.' She knew how tired I was and looked at me apologetically. 'He's a temporary resident.'

'OK,' I sighed, pulling my stethoscope out of my pocket and dropping it down onto the desk. I slumped back down into my chair. 'Show him in.'

'Temporary resident' is the phrase doctors use to describe a patient who does not live in the area and who is not a normal client of the practice. Bilbury, being so close to the coast, has more than its fair share of 'temporary residents' and in the summer it isn't unknown for half the patients at a surgery to be strangers.

The latecomer was in his sixties. He wore a heavy tweed three piece suit, a checked green and brown woollen shirt with button down collar points, a plain green woollen tie and a pair of highly polished brown brogues. His half moon gold framed spectacles gave him an academic air.

I vaguely waved a hand in the direction of the chair on the other side of the desk.

'Are you staying round here long?' I asked him after we had exchanged the usual formalities.

He mentioned the name of a well-known local hotel. 'I've been down for a few days break,' he told me. 'But I've got to be back at work tomorrow.' He spoke slowly and deliberately but rather loudly as though used to speaking to children. I wondered if he was a school master, though to be honest he seemed a little old. His nose was richly veined and he had a large, harmless lipoma growing out of the top of his balding head.

'What can I do for you?'

'I beg your pardon?'

'How can I help you?'

The latecomer leant forwards in his chair, frowned as though about to say something and then leant back again.

I waited.

'I'm sorry,' he apologised. 'My brain isn't as fast as it used to be.'

'That's O.K. Take your time. Tell me what's been worrying you.'

He glowered at me. 'Why should I tell you?'

'Er... I'm a doctor,' I mumbled. I waved a hand around, indicating the shelves piled high with books and medicines, the horsehair examination couch with the stuffing coming out of it and the eye test chart. 'This is my surgery.'

The latecomer looked around, as though seeing the room for the first time. 'I'm sorry,' he apologised, unexpectedly. 'That's what I came about. My memory is not what it was. The old grey matter seems to be getting a bit porridge-like.'

'If you're going back home then you should perhaps go and see your own doctor,' I suggested. 'You need some tests doing.'

'Can't you do them? You're a doctor aren't you?' I sighed silently.

'Take seven from one hundred!' I told him.

'Why?'

'It's a test for your brain.'

'Ninety something.'

'Can you be more precise?'

'Ninety two?'

'And seven from that?'

'Seventy? Seventy seven?' He waved a hair airily as though we both knew the answer didn't really matter. He was clearly suffering from senile dementia. 'Can you tell me the name of the Prime Minister?' I asked him.

'Why do you want to know? Don't *you* know?'

'Yes.' I said patiently. 'I know. But I want to see if you know. It's another test.'

'Churchill.' said the latecomer, without hesitation.

'Can you stay around in the village for a few more days?' I asked him. 'If you really want me to check you out I need more time.'

'I've got to go back.' he said. 'I'm in court tomorrow.'

'Oh.' I said. 'I'm sorry. Why? What... er... ?' I wondered what on earth he'd done. Exposed himself? Some innocent fraud? I felt sorry for him.

'I'm a judge.'

I went cold when he told me.

And even now I still feel cold when I think about it. I often wonder if he's still sitting on a bench somewhere, handing out judgements, making decisions about people's lives. A man who cannot do simple sums and who still thinks that Churchill is Prime Minister.

I don't want to know if he is still sitting on a bench and passing judgement. Patient-doctor confidentiality means that there is absolutely nothing I can do about it.

# FASHION CONSCIOUS

A month or so ago I read an interview with a professional cricketer who said that his favourite hobby was buying new clothes.

He confessed that he spent all his free time (and available money) on shopping for new shirts, trousers, jackets and suits.

This worried me rather a lot for I had always assumed that choosing and buying clothes was an essentially female activity. As far as I am concerned I wear clothes to keep me warm and dry and protect me from the elements. My only other criterion when choosing clothes is that they must have lots of pockets. I know that women never understand this essentially male craving for pockets but it is, nevertheless, important. Given a choice between a fashionable jacket in an agreeable colour with no pockets and an ill cut, nauseating looking jacket with plenty of pockets I would choose the ill cut, nauseating looking jacket with pockets every time.

But for a while the other day I harboured the fear that my simple view might be out-of-date, that men might be changing their views of clothes and that a growing number might be adopting a viewpoint that I had, in the past, always regarded as essentially feminine.

My experiences in the changing rooms at the Leisure Centre in Barnstaple really depressed me.

First, there were three school boys who were getting changed to go swimming. They were all around twelve or thirteen-years-old and you might have expected that they would have been talking about girls, football or racing drivers.

But they weren't.

Their sole topic of conversation revolved around the colour, size, shape, make and style of their footwear.

One of the schoolboys had just purchased a new pair of training shoes for which he (or, more accurately, his mother and father I suspect) had paid the sort of money for which one could, just a little while ago, have bought a perfectly decent *motor car!* The last time I looked, training shoes were called pumps or plimsolls and they came in black or white and cost no more than a hamburger. I doubt if any one I knew in my teens had the faintest idea who had *made* their pumps. The kids I was at school with would have laughed at the idea of arguing the merits of one pump manufacturer versus another.

But, I discovered that it isn't just teenagers who are now obsessed with what they wear. On the other side of the changing room there were two fellows in their late twenties who were getting ready to play badminton. They were obsessed with the cut of their trousers and they seemed genuinely interested in whether turn-ups were in or out of fashion! They talked knowledgeably and at length about gussets and linings and pleats and I found it all deeply disturbing.

When I was growing up things were very simple. Trousers, which were grey, had turn-ups and jeans, which were blue, did not. No male with his fair share of testosterone would be seen dead worrying in public about the *cut* of his trousers!

The final straw was a conversation I heard between two men who were getting changed for a karate class. They were tall and well-built and I felt confident that they at least would be talking about some healthy sporting activity. They weren't. One of the karate practitioners had just bought a new outfit and he was showing his companion the stitching and the material on his coloured belt.

That was bad enough. But what made it worse was that his companion was *interested!*

I hurried home from Barnstaple in a deep state of depression and was comforted slightly when I found that in the Duck and Puddle Thumper and Frank were arguing about whether the barmaid at the Gravediggers' Rest had a bigger bosom than Kay, our district nurse.

'Do you know who made your wellington boots?' I asked Thumper.

He looked at me as if I had gone mad. 'No.'

'Have your trousers got turn-ups on?' I asked Frank.

'I don't know.'

'What sort of belt do you use?' I asked Peter.

'Baler twine.'

Suddenly, I felt better.

I do like living in Bilbury.

# WAYNE WELLARD

People who live in towns always regard sheep as stupid animals. But sheep aren't at all stupid. They are certainly stubborn, they may be selfish and they are without doubt among the most determined of creatures, but they have more native intelligence than many human beings. Thumper Robinson seriously reckons that he has never met a policeman or a politician with the intelligence of a sheep.

Sheep have an outstanding ability to forge strong and lasting relationships and a burning curiosity. They also have very good memories. When I got the lawnmower out this year, for the first spring cut of the season, the sheep pricked up their ears, stared at me, studied the mower, looked at one another and then immediately responded by racing around to the spot in the field where I always dump the grass cuttings. They like eating freshly cut grass cuttings – I suppose it cuts down the work involved in eating! It had been six months since they had seen or heard the mower but they immediately knew what it meant!

Our five pet sheep, Lizzie, Petula, Cynthia, Sarah-Louise and Miss Houdini, all saved from a rendezvous with mint sauce, are spoilt rotten. Four of them were bottle fed from birth and since they still get one digestive biscuit each most days (they don't like any other types of biscuit half as much, though they did express some enthusiasm for chocolate finger biscuits last Christmas) they all greet any visitor with undisguised, unlimited enthusiasm.

Walk into the average sort of field where the average sort of sheep are grazing and they will, in the interests of self-preservation, run away from you.

But if you walk into a field where our five pet sheep are grazing they will run towards you at a startling pace.

In addition to this affection for human beings and digestive biscuits, they have acquired some rather unusual habits.

They don't like getting wet (we had a shelter built for them and if it rains they run in out of the rain quicker than you or I could put up an umbrella) and they hate mud. When we took them to be dipped one autumn neither Sarah-Louise nor Petula would walk through the muddy patch at the approach to the dip. Both looked down at it and backed away from it. They had to be carried across the quagmire.

I also have a strong suspicion that our sheep have acquired a sense of malicious mischief.

For example, last Wednesday the five sheep had more than a little fun with Wayne Wellard the farrier. Wayne Wellard was in the field putting some new shoes on Lightning, a horse who has been living in a spare stable at Bilbury Grange for a while.

Wayne Wellard is built along the lines of a small building and wherever he goes he is accompanied by his dog called Kamir. I was once stupid enough to ask him why he had given an Indian sounding name to a dog.

'Try shouting it out loud!' suggested the farrier, with a grin. I was called away to the telephone just as Wayne Wellard arrived, but since apart from Lightning herself the only animals in the field were the five sheep I didn't think anything about it. Fifteen minutes later I went back out to check that all was well and I heard an unmistakeable cry for help coming from the field. The cries were coming from somewhere behind the stable so I vaulted over the fence and ran round the corner to see what was going on. I could hardly believe my eyes.

There, standing with his back to the stable, his hands held up in front of him and a look of sheer terror on his face, was Wayne Wellard. Kamir was cowering behind him. And in front of them both were our five sheep. Cynthia and Petula were standing on their hind legs and resting their front legs on Wayne Wellard's thighs and Sarah-Louise, Lizzie and Miss Houdini were jumping up and down with excitement just behind them.

'Help!' cried Wayne. 'Get these bloody sheep off me!'

I put my hand into my coat pocket and found a few pieces of broken biscuit. When I called them, the sheep turned and raced towards me.

'Thank heavens for that!' said Wayne Wellard, sounding relieved. 'I've never been so terrified in all my life. I thought the damned things were going to eat me alive!' His dog whimpered pitifully.

'They're only sheep!' I pointed out, feeding them bits of biscuit. Lizzie jumped up and got one of her front legs caught in my coat pocket. I bent down and disentangled her.

'They're a menace!' insisted Wayne. 'There should be a law about sheep molesting people and their dogs.' He brushed some dirt and straw off his overalls and glowered at the sheep.

I couldn't help smiling. 'I can see the headline now!' I told him. 'Farrier claims sheep worried his dog.'

Wayne Wellard didn't say anything for a moment and then he half smiled. 'It's not funny,' he muttered defensively.

But it was.

# IRIS, MILO AND DAPHNE

Occasionally, we all misjudge people we hardly know. We hear things about them, we make assumptions and we come to conclusions based on hearsay, prejudice and gossip. Those of us who live in villages are, I suspect, more susceptible to this fault than anyone else for we are constantly exposed to stories, anecdotes and half truths about our neighbours.

Take Iris, for example, who lives right on the edge of Bilbury and who telephoned me on Monday. I have met her only half a dozen times and I have heard nothing but bad about her but this week she surprised me. Peter Marshall, who runs the village shop and is himself something of a master at being somewhere else when it is his turn to buy the drinks, claims that she is one of the meanest women in the county. I don't think I have ever heard anyone say anything nice about her.

In summer her cottage has lupins in the garden and a pink climbing rose round the door.

The beauty of her cottage is, however, rather spoilt by the fact that it has a rusting corrugated iron roof where the thatch used to be. Iris is reputed to have discovered that her insurance premium would fall dramatically if she had iron instead of reed on her roof and so when her thatch needed repairing she is said not to have hesitated before choosing the expedient, if ugly, alternative.

Doctors get a lot of very strange requests but I rather think that the first call I received from Iris ranks as one of the oddest I ever received.

When she telephoned, Iris sounded extremely anxious.

'It's Milo,' she said. 'I'm worried about him. He hasn't eaten for days. Would you come round and have a look at him?'

I didn't know she shared her cottage with anyone called Milo (her children have long since grown up and got as far away from home as they could and Iris's husband died of a rare vitamin deficiency while still in his late thirties - Frank, the landlord at the Duck and Puddle says that Iris regards spending money on food as rather akin to wasting it, arguing that there is little point in spending good money on a commodity that will, within hours, be nothing more than sewage) but before I could ask her for more information she had put the telephone down.

I left my lunch to congeal and raced off to see what was the matter. As I drove off I felt tired and depressed and full of despair. Over the weekend a young farm labourer had died in an accident and I had been the one who had to break the news to Daphne, his wife.

When I got there Milo turned out to be a Venus Fly Trap. A plant.

'He usually eats flies,' said Iris. 'I save a fortune on fly sprays.' She poked at one of his clearly empty leaf pouches.

'But he just hasn't been eating.'

'Why on earth did you ring me?' I asked, more bewildered than angry. 'I'm a doctor!' The call was so absurd that I just could not feel cross with her.

'I could hardly ring the vet, could I?' snorted Iris, with undeniable logic. 'And the people from the garden centre don't do house calls.'

I picked up a dead insect from the windowsill and tickled the fly trap with it. Hungrily, the fly trap opened a pouch and accepted the meal.

'You'll just have to try feeding it by hand,' I told her. 'Dead flies morning and night for a week.' I know nothing about house plants but if you say things with conviction it is easy to assume the air of an expert.

I turned as I was about to leave. 'Why do you call it Milo?'

'It's a Venus fly trap,' explained Iris wearily. 'Haven't you heard of the Venus de Milo?'

I hadn't thought of her as a person with a sense of humour. I smiled faintly and nodded my appreciation.

'While you're here,' said Iris, 'there's something I want you to take.' She walked over to the sideboard upon which there lay a thick brown envelope. She picked it up and handed it to me. It was unsealed and I peeped inside. It was full of bank notes.

'It's for Daphne King,' she said. 'I know what it's like to be widowed young. She'll be able to use that.' She stared at me. 'But you're not to tell her where it came from. I don't want everyone thinking I'm a soft touch.'

# THE ANNIVERSARY SURPRISE

Dennis Bride is not a regular in the Duck and Puddle. To be perfectly honest since their arrival a year or two ago neither he nor his wife, Ivy, have fitted into the village terribly well. Dennis has a rather important executive position (no one is sure precisely what) which takes him up to London two or three days a week.

Ivy is, to use a rather old-fashioned but eminently serviceable phrase, a bit stuck up. Her family have always had money and I think she finds it genuinely difficult to talk to 'ordinary' people like Frank, the publican, Peter the shopkeeper, Thumper (how on earth can I describe what Thumper does in a couple of words?) and me. She rides side saddle, wears a headscarf with beagles on it and speaks as though she's got a mouth full of ripe Victoria plums.

So we were all surprised when Dennis suddenly appeared just over a week ago, took out his wallet, and bought a round of drinks.

'It's my wedding anniversary on Friday,' he told us, when Frank had done his serious stuff with the optics and the beer pump and had poured Dennis his low calorie orange juice. 'My wife thinks I've forgotten - I nearly always do - but I thought it would be rather nice to have some people in from the village to help celebrate the occasion.'

I have to confess that none of us looked particularly excited by this. Thumper, Frank and Peter all looked as if they would have been more enthusiastic if invited to attend an evening of Welsh choral singing, meet with the local temperance society or join an insurance underwriting syndicate and although I tried hard to hide my feelings I don't think I was entirely successful. I've never had much of a soft spot for Ivy and the only genuine emotion I feel for Dennis is pity for his life seems to me to consist of long dull patches interspersed with periods of terminal boredom.

'I've got a firm of caterers coming over from Taunton,' said Dennis. 'And maybe you, Frank, would help us out with the drinks?'

'What did you have in mind?' asked Frank, with about as much enthusiasm as a politician invited to make a decision.

'Happy to leave that in your hands,' said Dennis. 'Whatever you think. You're the expert.'

'What did you plan on spending?' asked Frank.

'Open cheque,' said Dennis, using words which brought a glow to Frank's cheeks and a sparkle to his eyes.

'Right!' said Frank, enthusiastically. 'I should think I could help you out with that.'

Thumper, interest aroused, looked up. 'Friday, you said?'

Dennis nodded. 'But I don't want Ivy to find out about it. I want it to be a surprise.'

'She thinks you've forgotten it's your anniversary!' said Peter Marshall, dripping with understanding.

'Absolutely!' agreed Dennis. 'She'll be sitting there by the fire and then we'll all troop in and have a party. It'll be a good opportunity for us both to get to know everyone in the village.'

We arranged that at about eight o'clock on Friday evening Dennis would call in at the Duck and Puddle on his way back from London and we would then follow him back home. The booze would be packed into the back of Thumper's truck and the caterers would turn up at around nine. Everyone promised to make sure that Ivy didn't find out what was planned; since no one ever spoke to her this did not seem to be an unduly arduous responsibility.

On Friday evening everything seemed to go according to plan. Dennis arrived at 7.45 p.m. and we followed him back home in a straggly procession of trucks and tractors. We all parked in the lane and walked up to the house so as not to give the game away.

Dennis put his key in the front door lock and turned round to check that we were all there. We smiled encouragement at him. We were all carrying cases of alcohol. Frank had done us proud.

'I'm home, dear!' cried Dennis, walking briskly down the hall and into a spacious and elegantly furnished hallway. We all tip toed along behind him.

Ivy, her hair deliberately and carefully tousled, her face made up in what Thumper later described as a 'tarty' sort of way, responded to this greeting and tottered into view on pencil heeled black shoes. She was carrying two glasses of wine and dressed only in a pair of black fishnet stockings and a rather too small black and red basque over the top of which her ample bosom flowed like bubbling champagne. Behind her, in the dining room, I could see that the table had been set for a cosy, candle-lit anniversary dinner for two.

It was immediately clear that our arrival was something of a surprise to her.

'I've brought a few people from the village for dinner,' stuttered Dennis.

Ivy fainted.

'It was a good job you were there,' said Dennis, gratefully, when I had loosened his wife's clothing and helped him carry her upstairs to bed.

I did not like to point out that if I, and the rest of us, had not been there I probably would not have been needed.

Downstairs the pop of another cork was greeted with cries of approval.

# THE DISCLAIMER

I was fast asleep one night when I was woken by the sound of the telephone.

'Hello?' I mumbled.

'Is that the doctor?'

I said it was. I was still working as a general practitioner at the time.

'This is the duty sergeant at the police station,' said a voice I didn't recognise. 'Sorry to bother you, doctor, but our usual police surgeon has been taken ill with food poisoning and we're rather stuck. We wondered if you could help us out?'

'Me?'

'There is a fee,' said the sergeant. 'And we'd be extremely grateful. We've got a gentleman here who has been charged with a serious driving offence. The breathalyser suggests that he's been drinking rather heavily. We've offered him the choice of giving us a blood sample or a urine sample and he's chosen to give us a blood sample.'

'Oh,' I said. I could see their problem. If they couldn't find a doctor to take the blood sample the charges against the man would, presumably, have to be dropped.

Rather reluctantly I agreed to go.

I woke Patsy, told her where I was going, got dressed, got into the car and drove to the police station.

It was a terrible night. The wind was howling and the rain was lashing down. Pieces of branch were strewn all over the road.

It took me forty minutes to get from Bilbury Grange to the police station. Normally, the journey would have taken no more than half that time.

The police sergeant on duty greeted me with a smile and something that was a cross between a wave and a salute. He took me into the medical room where two police constables were waiting with a large, red-faced and bad-tempered looking man. The room was equipped with a cheap but sturdy looking metal desk, two steel framed plastic chairs and an examination couch.

The police sergeant gave me a form to complete and I asked the prisoner a few questions to confirm that he was willing to allow me to take a sample of his blood. He said he was.

When the form filling was finished with the policeman handed me a small packet that contained a syringe, a needle and two small containers for the blood sample. One sample, explained the sergeant, would be given to the prisoner. The other sample would be sent to the police laboratory.

'Would you please take off your coat and roll up your sleeve?' I asked the prisoner.

The man stared at me belligerently and scowled. I repeated my request.

'No,' he said, bluntly. 'I won't.'

'But you've just agreed...,' I reminded him.

'I said you could take blood,' he said. 'But not from my arm.'

He ended this sentence with a loud hiccup.

I stared at him uncomprehendingly.

'You can take it from here!' he announced, suddenly unzipping his trousers and producing a part of his body which I had never previously regarded as offering a particular popular or suitable site for venepuncture.

I stared at the man and at the small and shrunken organ which he was holding.

'The law doesn't say *you* can choose where you take the blood from,' announced the man, as though he knew what he was talking about.

I turned to the sergeant. 'Doesn't it?' I whispered.

The sergeant shrugged. 'I don't know, doctor!' he admitted.

'I've been doing this job for twelve years and I've never come across anything like this before.'

'Come on!' said the man, tauntingly waving his organ at me. 'Take your damned blood!'

I took the sterilised syringe out of its packet and fitted the sterilised needle onto the end of it.

And then I had one of those flashes of inspiration which usually arrive about a day and a half too late.

'If you want me to take the blood from there just drop your trousers while I prepare this disclaimer for you to sign,' I said. I took a pen from my pocket and took a blank sheet of writing paper from a wire tray on the top of the desk.

'What disclaimer?' demanded the man. He had not dropped his trousers. Indeed, he was now holding two hands across his opened fly.

'Just in case anything goes wrong,' I told him. 'Taking blood from that particular site can occasionally result in gangrene and eventual amputation.'

The belligerent prisoner stared at me. 'Amputation?' He winced.

'It's not a terribly big risk,' I told him. 'But you have to sign to say that you accept the risk.'

'I'm not signing!' said the man, backing away from me nervously. I don't think I've ever seen anyone change their mind quite so quickly. He threw off his coat and rolled up his shirt sleeve. 'Here!' he said, holding out his bare arm, complete with a nice, juicy looking vein. 'Take it from here!'

# THE KITCHEN CHAIRS

We had visitors from London last weekend.

Tony and Yvette are both in the restaurant trade and they are both huge. Tony, a chef at an Italian restaurant weighs at least sixteen stones and Yvette, a waitress, must be even heavier.

Halfway through their visit Yvette sat down on one of our kitchen chairs and ended up sitting on the floor amidst a muddle of splintered wood. The chair, an old piece of pine furniture which we had found at the back of the barn, had simply decided that enough was enough and had given up the ghost.

Patsy and I decided that rather than buy something new, which would look distinctly out of place in our kitchen, we would visit Patchy Fogg's antique shop and see if he had anything suitable as a replacement. We also thought that we would be able to buy something for less money at Patchy's than at any of the local furniture stores.

'I can let you have this set of four Victorian rosewood chairs for £135,' said Patchy, caressing the back of one of the chairs he was offering us.

Patsy and I looked at each other.

'That's rather more than we intended to pay,' said Patsy, with a frown.

'It's only for the kitchen,' I pointed out. 'Haven't you got something the same sort of age but a little cheaper?' I paused. 'Rather a lot cheaper actually.'

Patchy took his hat off and scratched the top of his head with simple, easy movement. Then, as though suddenly struck by a sudden thought, he put his hat back on again and disappeared through a door into a room that was packed from floor to ceiling with miscellaneous bits and pieces of furniture.

'I was going to put this into an auction in South Molton,' he said, reappearing and holding a plain, stripped pinewood kitchen chair out towards us. He examined a small, white label stuck onto the back of the chair. 'It's Victorian. I was going to put a reserve of £20 on it,' he told us. 'But for cash, without any commissions and so on, I can let you have it for £12.'

Patsy and I looked at the chair. It wasn't anything special to look at but it did look as though it would suit our kitchen.

I took the chair off him, found a space on the floor and put the chair down. I sat on it. It didn't break.

'It seems OK,' I said to Patsy.

'It looks quite nice,' said Patsy.

'But it is a little expensive,' I said.

Foggy sighed. '£10 then,' he said. 'But that's rock bottom. At £10 you're saving more than you're spending.' He reached out and fondled the chair. 'You could pay £50 for one like this in a London antique shop,' he murmured.

Patsy and I still didn't commit ourselves.

'Look,' said Foggy. 'I think I might have another one like it somewhere. Do you want me to have a look?'

Patsy and I exchanged glances. 'Yes, please.' I said.

Again, Patchy disappeared.

He reappeared a few moments later clutching a second chair.

'You can have the two for £17,' he said. 'I can't do any fairer than that.' He shook his head as though embarrassed by his own generosity. 'They should be going to the auction with a reserve of £20 each on them.'

I sat on the second chair.

'That means you're saving £23 on the two chairs,' he said. 'And you've saved £83 on what you'd have to spend in London.'

'It sounds very good value,' I agreed, by now totally confused.

'I'm too damned soft-hearted for this business,' sighed Patchy.

'Do you think you might find any more like them?' asked Patsy. 'If we're going to buy two it would be nice to put a set of four together eventually.'

Patchy rubbed his chin. 'At this price?'

I nodded.

Patchy shook his head. 'At this price I'm making a loss,' he said. 'I have to pay more than you're paying me!'

I took out my wallet and counted out £30. 'For four,' I said.

Patchy sucked in air. 'You should be in this business,' he said. He turned round. 'I'll go and have a look in the back and see what there is. But only because I like you both.'

Three or four minutes later we packed four chairs into the car.

'You've got a real bargain there,' said Patchy. He laughed. 'Do me a favour will you? Don't come back too soon! I can't afford to do too much business with you two!'

Patsy and I felt very pleased with ourselves.

Two days later Thumper Robinson called in to talk about some work he was doing on the stables.

'I see you've been to Jasper Bottomley's Furniture Warehouse,' said Thumper, sitting down on one of our chairs. 'They almost look like the real thing, don't they?' Patsy and I exchanged glances.

'What do you mean?' asked Patsy.

'We got them from Patchy Fogg,' I said. 'They're Victorian.'

Thumper put his head in his hands. 'How much did you pay?' he asked, a moment later.

I told him.

'Jasper brings them in as kits from Taiwan, has them glued together in Torrington and sells them for £4.99 each,' said Thumper

# A BUSY WEEK IN BILBURY

There's been so much happening this week in Bilbury that I hardly know where to start. On Monday Norman and Elsie Burrows had an argument over their false teeth which resulted in a small domestic disaster.

For twelve years now, ever since Elsie's teeth were eaten by one of Dr Brownlow's Doberman puppies, the two of them have shared a set of artificial dentures which Norman bought in 1956 from a dental technician in Bristol. (To be honest the man wasn't a proper dental technician. He earned his living as an undertaker but made false teeth in his spare time and, according to Norman, had quite a reputation in that part of the West Country).

When they go out to dinner they take it in turns to chew. Norman will usually start with the teeth (because they are his) but when he's finished eating his meat, he'll wrap the dentures up in his handkerchief and pass them on to Elsie (who will have been busy with her vegetables) so that she can chew her meat properly.

No one seems to know what caused the argument on Monday but Norman tried to snatch the dentures and ended up knocking them onto the floor and before anyone could stop her Dulcie Patterson had trodden on them.

All may not be lost, however, for Peter Marshall says he's got some special repair glue and he's going to try to mend the fractured dentures before Roy Pilton and Iris Martinhoe get married on Saturday.

On Tuesday evening Patchy Fogg called in at the Duck and Puddle to tell us that he'd come third in a golf tournament at Kentisbury. Since Patchy only started to play golf six months ago we were all terribly impressed and several of us bought him drinks.

Early on Wednesday morning Peter Marshall rushed out of his shop and announced to the world that he had been burgled and that someone had stolen his alarm clock. As you can imagine this caused a considerable amount of excitement in the village and P.C. Wren was summoned to take statements from everyone who was in a fit state to make them.

On Wednesday afternoon Harry Tattersall arrived back in Bilbury in a taxi and was promptly turned round by his wife Trudy who was the only one of the pair who remembered that when he left the house for a business meeting in Belgium last Thursday, Harry had taken their car. He had left the car at Heathrow Airport. Harry is terribly absent-minded and once phoned home to say that he was in Madrid and could Trudy please tell him what he was doing there. On one famous occasion he got as far as Istanbul with no money, no passport, no luggage and only carpet slippers on his feet.

Late on Wednesday evening Peter Marshall called the police again and reported that the burglar who had stolen his alarm clock had left a bomb behind his bedside table. P.C. Wren, who, despite pressure from Peter, was reluctant to call the bomb squad all the way from London, bravely investigated and discovered that the ticking was caused by Peter's alarm clock which must have fallen off the table the night before.

On Thursday Roy Pilton came into the pub and said he was having second thoughts about getting married. When he'd had a few pints of Frank's best bitter he said he'd marry Iris if, when he tossed a coin, it came up heads three times running.

The first three tosses were all tails so Thumper said they couldn't be counted and Roy had to carry on. Eventually, after tossing the coin 18 times it came up heads three times running and to everyone's relief Roy swore that he'd go ahead with the wedding. The relief was occasioned by the fact that Roy is 42, Iris is 39, they have three teenage children and two grandchildren and they've been living together for 19 years.

On Friday, Patchy came into the pub looking very penitent and admitted that although it was true that he had come third in the Kentisbury Golf Tournament there had only been three entrants and he had taken 37 strokes more than the player who'd taken second place. He admitted that he had only shared this news with us when he had discovered that the full scores are to be printed in next week's edition of the *Barnstaple, Bideford and Bilbury Herald.* Thumper said we'd all forgive him this slight deceit on condition that he bought drinks for all of us and rather to everyone's surprise he did.

On Saturday Roy and Iris got married and despite all the business with the alarm clock Peter Marshall had still found time to mend Norman and Elsie's false teeth and so they were able to enjoy themselves as usual.

# INDISPENSABLE

Most people eventually lose much of the accent they had as children if they move to a new locality and stay there long enough. Britons who emigrate to America or Canada usually come home speaking with a noticeable transatlantic twang. And even the Irish usually lose much of their brogue when they've lived in England for a few years.

But Evan Jones who lives on the outskirts of Bilbury and operates a one man taxi service into and out of Barnstaple is the proverbial exception who proves the rule. Evan has lived in Bilbury for longer than he or anyone else can remember but still speaks with such a broad native Welsh accent that most local people who do not know him well have to ask him to repeat everything he says several times. His accent is so broad that holiday-makers are frequently confused and assume that they cannot understand him because he is speaking in traditional Devonian.

I bumped into Evan late on Tuesday evening when I called into the Duck and Puddle to appease my rumbling stomach with one of Gilly Parson's cheese and mushroom pies. I've been a firm fan of Gilly's cooking ever since I moved to Bilbury. I was still working as the village doctor at the time and I was on my way home from delivering Mrs Bassett's seventh baby (when I claim the responsibility for 'delivering' the baby I am being unduly generous to myself for Mrs Bassett is such an accomplished mother that my role was confined to cutting the cord and accepting a large glass of very good whisky from Mr Bassett) and I found Evan slumped on the bar with his head in his hands and an untouched pint going flat on the bar in front of him. It's not like Evan to let a pint of beer go flat.

Beside Evan sat Dr Brownlow.

Dr Brownlow is the doctor who founded the practice I was running. Retired from medical practice (but not by any means retired from life) he had celebrated his birthday two weeks earlier but still looked fitter than many men twenty years younger than he was. Sitting upright on his bar-stool he was sipping his customary glass of malt whisky with obvious enjoyment.

Some people drink alcohol because they want to get drunk and forget their worries and a few drink the stuff because they are thirsty but Dr Brownlow drinks it because he likes the taste. Frank buys Dr Brownlow's favourite malt whisky by the case.

'I'm shattered, doc,' Evan sighed, when I asked him what was troubling him. (I knew that I had become a local in the village when I found that I could understand him). 'I had a funeral in Combe Martin on Monday and a wedding in Lynton on Tuesday and I've done seven trips into Barnstaple today.' Evan normally shared the taxi work with Peter Marshall, who keeps the village shop in Bilbury, but Peter's car had been off the road for a few weeks and so Evan had, for many in the village, been the only means of communication with the outside world.

'Why don't you say 'no' occasionally?'

Evan looked up at me sharply, as though I'd suggested that he give up beer, cigarettes or breathing. 'Say 'no'?' He looked across at Dr Brownlow as though expecting support.

'No one is indispensable,' Dr Brownlow pointed out.

Evan raised a doubting eyebrow.

Dr Brownlow took a sip at his whisky and sighed with delight. 'The church graveyard is full of people who thought they were indispensable,' he said wisely.

Evan was clearly unconvinced.

'If you work too hard you'll make yourself ill,' I warned him, prosaically.

Suddenly, Dr Brownlow climbed off his stool, leant over the bar and lifted a bowl of washing up water up onto the bar top. 'Put your hand into that,' he ordered Evan.

Obediently, Evan did as he was told though the water looked none too clean. People who have lived in Bilbury for more than a few years always do whatever Dr Brownlow tells them to do.

When I first came to work in Bilbury I was told a story about a woman who hadn't been out of bed for eleven years. Dr Brownlow had ordered her to stay there during an attack of flu. He had told her not to budge until he told her otherwise but had then forgotten to go back. At first I thought the story was apocryphal. These days I'm not so sure.

'Pull your hand out of the water.'

Once again Evan did what he was told.

'Now look at the size of the hole that you've left behind.' said Dr Brownlow.

Evan stared at the bowl of water blankly.

*'That's* how indispensable you are.' Dr Brownlow told him.

# THE CRICKET CLUB DINNER

You will not be surprised to hear that the Bilbury Village Cricket Club usually holds its annual dinner at the Duck and Puddle.

Frank, the landlord, puts in an order for an extra couple of barrels of best bitter. Gilly, his partner in life and business, bakes a few dozen pies. And Peter at the village shop lets us have his left over Christmas crackers and Christmas paper serviettes at half price. (Peter always stocks very flimsy paper serviettes that look quite seasonal because they have scalloped edges and holly decorations but which are tissue paper thin and provide about as much protection from a spoonful of gravy or a dollop of custard as would a spider's web. I gather he buys them very cheaply from a wholesaler in Leeds who bought a warehouse full of them in 1946). Maisie Falmouth, the club treasurer's wife, hammers out some menus on her 1926 Royal sit up and beg typewriter. (The typewriter she uses, which once belonged to the late Arthur Appleyard, the author of the best-selling 'My Days at Sea' and undoubtedly one of Bilbury's best-known literary figures, lost its 'e' in 1987 and so since then Gilly has been under strict instructions to try her best to provide dishes that don't have an 'e' in them. This is even more difficult than it sounds. Try it if you don't believe me.)

This year, however, the club's four man committee (which basically consists of Kenneth, the club honorary vice president, because none of the other committee members is ever sober for long enough to make any sensible contributions to the proceedings) decided that we should hold our annual dinner at the Ritz-Carlton hotel; one of the very few establishments in North Devon which can boast both a full-time doorman who wears a top hat and a green tail coat and a porter who is employed to clean the guests' shoes while they sleep.

The man who is employed to clean the guests' shoes is called Carl Kassenbaum, by the way, and he has a very simple system to ensure that the shoes he removes are put back outside the correct bedroom doors. Sometime you must remind me to tell you about the night that Thumper Robinson decided to 'help' Carl 'improve' his system and accidentally got a high court judge mixed up in a rather unpleasant divorce scandal.

To be honest none of us was terribly keen about this change in our annual routine but by the time we found out what was happening, Kenneth had booked the hotel dining room and it was too late to do anything about it because the hotel had written Kenneth a letter telling him that the booking deposit was non-refundable.

'It's a daft idea,' complained Thumper, who pointed out that whereas we could all drive home from the Duck and Puddle without any danger of being stopped by the police we would never all get back to Bilbury without attracting Mr Plod's attention.

'I've hired a coach!' countered Kenneth. 'The coach will pick us all up at the Duck and Puddle and when the dinner is over, the coach will take us all back to our cars at the Duck and Puddle. Then we can all drive ourselves home.'

Grudgingly, Thumper agreed that this plan would at least reduce our chances of ending the night blowing up police sponsored balloons. 'Where did you find a coach driver who was prepared to sit around for four or five hours?' I asked Kenneth.

'Peter Marshall agreed to do it,' said Kenneth. 'He's borrowing the school bus for the evening.'

No one could argue too much about that and so last Saturday evening at about half past seven we all put down our glasses at the Duck and Puddle, said goodbye to Frank and Gilly (Frank is a vice President of the club but, not surprisingly, he was in a bit of a huff and had refused to join us) and clambered into the coach.

'You can't come in here,' said Eugene Cudlipp, the doorman at the Ritz-Carlton, when we all climbed down from the coach and tried to shuffle into the hotel.

'Don't be silly, Tiny,' said Kenneth. 'We've booked the dining room for the cricket club dinner.' Eugene, who is six foot six inches tall, has been called 'Tiny' since he was fifteen.

'I'm sorry, Mr Falmouth,' said Tiny, who was clearly quite genuinely cut up about it all. 'You and Mr Petherick can come in, but none of the others.'

'What on earth do you mean?' demanded Kenneth. 'Why can Reggie and I come in when the rest can't?'

'Because you're the only two who are wearing ties,' explained Tiny. 'The hotel manager doesn't allow guests into the hotel if they aren't wearing ties.' He looked around at the rest of us as we clutched at our tie-less throats.

And daft as it sounds they wouldn't let us in.

Kenneth insisted that Tiny went and fetched the manager but he wouldn't budge.

So, in the end Peter took us back to the Duck and Puddle where Gilly cooked us all egg and chips and Frank refused to sell us any beer until we'd all combed our hair. Peter popped out and fetched some Christmas crackers and serviettes so only Maisie's menus were missing but since there's an 'e' in 'egg and chips' she wouldn't have been able to type that out anyway.

# THE CHRISTMAS FAYRE

The Bilbury Christmas Fayre may not be much compared to Disneyland but it's all we've got and every year it gives everyone a tremendous amount of pleasure.

America's Disneyland has its rides, its castles and a larger than life version of Mickey Mouse but the Bilbury Fayre has a proper old-fashioned coconut shy, a 'guess the weight of the cake' competition (Mrs Anstruthers always makes the cake and it is well-known now in the village that in order to stand a chance of winning first prize you have to double the first weight you thought of), a stall where you can win a goldfish if you can throw one of the rubber rings that are used for sealing jam jars over a pencil standing in a block of plasticine and a stall where you can rent three wooden balls and throw them, just for the hell of it, at four rows of redundant crockery. A banker from Manchester once put down a £20 note and stayed at the 'break a plate' stall for an hour and a half, breaking umpteen old plates and happily exorcising a year's accumulated strains and stresses. He was afterwards heard to claim that he had derived more relief from this ninety minutes of organised destruction than he had from two and a half years of extremely expensive psychoanalysis.

In my first year as a doctor in Bilbury I was honoured by being put in charge of the 'guess the number of peas in a teapot' stall. A small handwritten card pinned to the trestle table upon which my teapot stood informed competitors that the prize on offer was a 'flamingo pink' plastic shower caddy 'designed to hold soap, shampoo and sponge while you shower with complete freedom and confidence'.

Despite the fact that as far as I aware there was not one home in Bilbury which contained a fitted shower, this prize seemed surprisingly attractive to those villagers who regarded themselves as expert in the unusual and esoteric art of judging the pea capacity of a brown catering size teapot.

All things considered there is no doubt that the Christmas Fayre was, as usual, an enormous success and when I left at nine thirty, I was tired but contented for my stall alone had raised over £7 towards the Village Hall Dry Rot Fund, a noble attempt to raise enough money to enable the village hall to combat the ravages of a persistent and apparently insatiable fungus.

To be honest I would have left earlier, for since the fuses in the village hall blew up at Halloween all of our social events have been primarily afternoon affairs, but Mrs Pilkington told me that as custodian of the 'peas in the teapot' stall it was my responsibility to check the entries and find the winner.

'Fine,' I said. 'Have you got the correct answer?'

'What answer?' asked Mrs Pilkington.

'The number of peas there are in the teapot,' I explained.

'Oh no,' said Mrs Pilkington. 'You've got to count them yourself.'

In view of the lack of light I did my counting sitting in the car and it was pitch black when I left. Since I was hungry and I knew that Patsy, who had been in charge of the 'toss a horseshoe over a wooden stake' stall, had gone over to Barnstaple with Kay to visit Elspeth Norwich who was still in hospital after her unfortunate accident with the patented automatic butter pat maker which she bought from an auction in Torrington, I decided to call in at the Duck and Puddle for a bite of something to eat.

'I'm glad you're here,' said Gilly. 'Would you call round on the Prestons? Mrs Preston rang half an hour ago and said it was urgent. She hoped you might pop in. They can't get hold of the doctor in Barnstaple.' The Prestons' cottage is only about five minutes away from the pub so I asked Gilly to cook me some chips, cut me half a dozen slices of bread and butter and put a couple of eggs out for frying while I popped over there to see what was the matter.

'It's our Henry,' said Mrs Preston, opening the door and ushering me in. 'He's been in bed for three days with a bit of a cold.'

'Right,' I said. 'Let's have a look at him, then!'

'I took Simon to the Fayre,' said Mrs Preston, as she led the way upstairs. Simon is her other son. At nine he is two years older than Henry. 'We won a goldfish which Simon insisted that we gave to Henry.'

'That's nice,' I murmured.

'Well it was,' said Mrs Preston, opening the door to Henry's bedroom. Henry was sitting up in bed looking, I thought, rather pleased with himself. 'Simon insisted that we put the goldfish by Henry's bed so that he'd see it when he woke up.'

I still didn't guess what had happened.

'We haven't got a goldfish tank,' said Mrs Preston. 'So I put the fish into a glass of water,' she nodded towards a half empty drinking glass on Henry's bedside table. It clearly contained no goldfish.

'I can't see a goldfish,' I said, stupidly.

'No,' said Mrs Preston. 'Henry woke up feeling thirsty and took a drink out of the glass.'

And that is when I realised where the goldfish was.

'The goldfish is in my tummy,' said Henry, just in case I still hadn't worked it out. He looked very pleased with himself.

'Do you think he'll be all right?' asked Mrs Preston, anxiously.

I told her that my fears were entirely for the goldfish and asked her to ring Gilly and tell her to put my eggs in the frying pan.

# THE ANTIQUE TABLE

It's been a busy week in Bilbury.

I've been involved in something very illegal and I've spent all the money Patsy and I have on a table for Bilbury Grange.

It all started when Patchy Fogg came into the Duck and Puddle on Tuesday evening looking really miserable.

'What on earth's the matter with you?' asked Thumper. 'You look as though you've lost a Georgian silver sugar sifter and found a plastic tea spoon!'

'I'm in a quandary,' moaned Patchy. 'It's terrible. I really don't know what to do.'

Frank pulled him a pint of stout and handed him a packet of crisps, and armed with these life-saving essentials Patchy sat himself down at the bar.

'One of those interior decorators from London came into the shop today,' he told us. 'He saw that oak refectory table I've got, got himself all excited the way they do, and told me he wanted to buy it for a client in Kensington.'

'Sounds good so far,' said Thumper with a grin. 'He didn't knock you down too far on the price, did he?'

'Didn't even haggle,' said Patchy. 'Those guys never do. They're working on commission so the more they spend the more they make.' He pushed a handful of crisps into his mouth, crunched them to death and then washed them down with a long draught of stout.

'So where's your problem?' demanded Thumper. 'Sounds like a good day's work to me!'

'He wants the table for what he called a 'dining nook',' said Patchy. 'And apparently his client's 'dining nook' is nine inches shorter than my table.'

'Can't they knock a wall down or something?'

Patchy shook his head miserably. 'Apparently not,' he said. 'He wants me to take nine inches off the table before I deliver it.'

Now, at last, Frank, Thumper and I all understood Patchy's dilemma.

Patchy Fogg is a smooth operator, a fast talker and not above a little bit of chicanery. There probably aren't many things that he won't do to make a few bob.

But he does have a genuine and enduring love for antiques.

'What the hell am I to do?' he asked us, plaintively. 'I've had that table for nine months. It's a beautiful piece of work. I was beginning to abandon the idea of selling it at the price I need to get to give me a profit.' He crunched some more crisps and washed them down again with more stout. 'But it's a marvellous table. It came from a monastery in Yorkshire and it's absolutely genuine. Sixteenth century. It would be an act of vandalism to chop nine inches off the end just so that it will fit into some damned 'dining nook' in Kensington.'

'Can't you switch tables?' asked Thumper, clearly surprised that Patchy hadn't thought of it.

'Obvious thing to do,' agreed Patchy. 'My first thought. But I've got to deliver the damned table on Friday so I've got two days. I've got no chance of finding anything remotely like it.'

'Make a copy and chop nine inches off the copy,' said Thumper, bluntly.

Patchy looked at him rather wearily. 'I've got two days!' he said. 'Two days to make a sixteenth century oak refectory table?' He laughed but it was a hollow, tragic laugh.

'We'll give you a hand,' said Thumper. 'I've got some old oak planks that came out of a house in Parracombe and you must have some handmade nails.'

Patchy looked at him and then looked at Frank and me. For a few moments he didn't say anything. 'Would you?' he asked.

'Of course!' said Thumper. 'Anything to help a mate out.'

I swallowed hard. 'I'll help,' I agreed. 'I'd rather you sold him a fake than cut the end off a genuine antique table.'

'I dare say there'll be a drink in it for us ...,' said Frank with a grin.

'There certainly will!' said Patchy, enthusiastically.

So there and then Frank left Gilly in charge of the Duck and Puddle and while he and I and Thumper drove out to Thumper's place and started sorting out the oak planks, Patchy called in at his shop to measure the table and pick up some old handmade nails and wooden pegs.

It took us thirty hours to make the fake table and when we'd finished it looked so good that Frank had to turn away when Thumper got his saw and cut nine inches off the end of it. Frank said that even though it was a fake cutting it up was sacrilegious.

On Saturday, when Patchy got back from London, he rang to invite Thumper, Frank and me round to his place to help him celebrate. The interior decorator had paid him cash and Thumper and Frank looked very pleased with their share of the proceeds. I told Patchy that I'd talked it over with Patsy and that if he didn't mind we'd like to buy the original sixteenth century refectory table for Bilbury Grange and we'd be happy to have my cut of the profits as a discount.

Patchy said he'd be delighted and promised to deliver the table next Tuesday.

On our way back home Thumper told me that he had scratched an almost invisible mark on one of the legs just to be on the safe side.

'It's not that I don't trust Patchy,' he said. 'But sometimes temptation can be very difficult to resist when you're an antique dealer.'


*The End*

If you enjoy the Bilbury books, you may enjoy other books by the same author. For full details of over 100 books by Vernon Coleman, please see his author page on Amazon or http://www.vernoncoleman.com

# THE BILBURY CHRONICLES

## Vernon Coleman

The first in the Bilbury series of novels describing the adventures (and misadventures) of a young doctor who enters general practice as the assistant to an elderly and rather eccentric doctor in North Devon.

When he arrives in Bilbury, a small village on the edge of Exmoor, the young doctor doesn't realise how much he has to learn. And he soon discovers the true extent of his ignorance when he meets his patients.

There's Anne Thwaites who gives birth to her first baby in a field; Thumper Robinson who knows a few tricks that aren't in any textbook and Mike Trickle, a TV quiz show host who causes great excitement when he buys a house in the village.

Then there's elderly Dr Brownlow himself who lives in a house that looks like a castle, drives an old Rolls Royce and patches his stethoscope with a bicycle inner tube repair kit; Frank the inebriate landlord of the Duck and Puddle, and Peter who runs the local taxi, delivers the mail and works as the local undertaker.

There's Miss Johnson, the receptionist with a look that can curdle milk; Mrs Wilson the buxom district nurse and Len her husband who is the local policeman with an embarrassing secret.

'A delightful read. I was entranced for hours.' – *Miss S, Devon*
'I loved this book. Please send two more copies as soon as possible.' – *Mrs S, Nottingham*
'Wonderful. One of the best novels I've ever read.' – *Mr T, Leamington Spa*
'I enjoyed "The Bilbury Chronicles" more than any other book I've read for years. I am very much looking forward to the sequel.' – *Mrs G, Sunderland*

# BILBURY GRANGE

Vernon Coleman

The second novel in the Bilbury series. The Doctor and his wife
move to Bilbury Grange – a dream of a house with stone lions
guarding the front door, a Victorian, walled kitchen garden and a
coach house complete with clock tower. But the newly married
couple have no idea of the horrors that await them – crumbling
slates, rampant woodworm, creeping dry rot and, worst of all,
crooked builders all too ready to lend a hand. With money tight and
repair bills soaring the young couple have to find a way to make
ends meet.

But repairing Bilbury Grange isn't the only problem they face.
Rumours abound that a developer is about to build new houses and a
golf course in the village – and to top it all Thumper Robinson gets
arrested!

Somewhere, as all this is going on, the Doctor and Patsy find time
to adopt two young kittens and four young lambs.

'Captures the essence of old-fashioned village life where you never
needed to lock your door.' – *Western Evening Herald*
'A wonderful book for relaxing and unwinding…makes you want to
up roots and move to the rural heartland. – *Lincolnshire Echo*
'For sheer relaxing pleasure here's another witty tale from the doctor
whose prolific writings are so well known to many of us.' –
*Bookshelf*

# BILBURY REVELS

Vernon Coleman

The Bilbury series continues with this, the third novel set in the
idyllic Exmoor village.
Disaster strikes during a long, relentless storm which batters Bilbury
Grange, cuts off the village and blankets the whole area in a thick
covering of snow. The Doctor nearly loses his life (he is saved by his

faithful dog Ben) and the village schoolteacher loses her cottage roof.

The fun really starts when the villagers join together to raise money to repair the devastated cottage. Vernon Coleman describes an old-fashioned music hall evening (during which just about everything which can go wrong does go wrong), one of the funniest cricket matches ever to take place, and a village Produce Show where the locals compete (with some very surprising results) to find out who has grown the biggest and best vegetables.

And as if that wasn't enough the Doctor has to promote his first book. He travels to London, makes his first hilarious television appearance, and is invited to speak at a local village hall where things aren't quite what they seem to be.

Vernon Coleman's comic novels have been compared to Jerome K. Jerome's classic 'Three Men in a Boat'. Readers of the previous Bilbury books will love The Bilbury Revels. New readers be warned – you'll be hooked.

# THE VILLAGE CRICKET TOUR

Vernon Coleman

A novel describing the adventures and mishaps of a team of cricketers who spend two weeks of their summer holidays on a cricket tour of the West Country, and who make up in enthusiasm for what they may lack in skill.

'If anyone ever manages to bottle the essence of the village cricket he will very quickly scale the dizzy heights of personal fortune. In the meantime we read and write about it in pursuit of understanding. Seminal reading here includes Selincourt and Blunden and should now embrace Vernon Coleman's latest offering, a whimsical piece about the peregrinations of a village team on its summer tour...all the characters are here, woven together by a raft of anecdotes and reminiscences and a travelogue of some of the most picturesque spots in the south west.' – *The Cricketer*

'Describes in hilarious fashion the triumphs and disasters of a Midlands teams tour of the West Country and there is not a little of Jerome K. Jerome in Mr Coleman's style. ' – *Worcester Evening News*

'I enjoyed it immensely. He has succeeded in writing a book that will entertain, a book that will amuse and warm the cockles of tired hearts. And what a change it makes from the wearisome cluckings of the current crop of cricket books with their grinding pomposity and, in many cases, their staggering lack of craftsmanship and originality. ' – *Punch*

'A delightful book which also highlights some of the most spectacular scenery in Cornwall and Devon.' – *The Cornishman*

'Vernon Coleman is obviously a man who has enjoyed his cricket and over the years has committed to memory the many characters he has seen playing the game. He weaves them into the story as he charts the progress of his team's tour of Devon and Cornwall. The tale captures club cricket as everyone imagines it should be.' – *Falmouth Packet*

'Coleman is a very funny writer. It would be a pity if cricketers were the only people to read this book.' – *This England*

# THE MAN WHO INHERITED A GOLF COURSE

Vernon Coleman

Trevor Dukinfield, the hero of this delightful novel, is a young, not very successful journalist. Completely out of the blue, Trevor receives a letter informing him that he has inherited a golf course from an uncle he never knew he had.

You might think that this would have been greeted by Trevor as good news. Indeed, Trevor *did* treat it as good news until he heard about the two small snags which accompanied his good fortune.

First, in order to keep the golf club under the rules of his uncle's will, Trevor must play a round of golf in less than 100 strokes. Second, he has to find a partner to help him beat two bankers in a match play competition. Not particularly stringent conditions you might think - except that Trevor has never played a round of golf in his life, unless you count an hour spent on a crazy golf course in Weston-super-Mare.

'Another witty volume from the doctor who has successfully turned from medical topics to novel writing. The...mix of anecdotes and moments of sheer farce make for an absorbing read.' – *Lancashire Evening Telegraph*
...another delightful and amusing story. I rate this one as the best of his twelve novels so far. His fans will lap it up.' – *Sunday Independent*

# MRS CALDICOT'S CABBAGE WAR

Vernon Coleman

Thelma Caldicot was married to her husband for thirty dull and boring years. Then completely out of the blue, two police officers arrived at Thelma's house to break some sad news. That afternoon, while her husband was at a cricket match, she had become a widow.

Her ambitious son Derek soon appears on the scene, determined to interfere in every aspect of his mother's life. After thirty years of being dominated by her husband, it looks as though Thelma's son is about to step into his shoes and continue the good work.

But then something happens to Thelma Caldicot. After years of being pushed around and told what to do, she takes charge of her life and fights back.

Mrs Caldicot's Cabbage War is the poignant, warm and often funny story of an ordinary women who finally decides to stand up for herself.

'...a splendid, relaxing read...' – *Sunday Independent*
Thank you so much for Mrs Caldicott's Cabbage War. All your books are great. – *Mrs N*

Printed in Great Britain
by Amazon